D1315294

INSIDE
OBAMA'S
BRAIN

INSIDE OBAMA'S BRAIN

—

SASHA ABRAMSKY

PORTFOLIO

PORTFOLIO

Published by the Penguin Group

Penguin Group (USA) Inc., 375 Hudson Street, New York, New York 10014, U.S.A. ▪
Penguin Group (Canada), 90 Eglinton Avenue East, Suite 700, Toronto, Ontario, Canada
M4P 2Y3 (a division of Pearson Penguin Canada Inc.) ▪ Penguin Books Ltd, 80 Strand,
London WC2R 0RL, England ▪ Penguin Ireland, 25 St. Stephen's Green, Dublin 2, Ireland
(a division of Penguin Books Ltd) ▪ Penguin Books Australia Ltd, 250 Camberwell Road,
Camberwell, Victoria 3124, Australia (a division of Pearson Australia Group Pty Ltd) ▪
Penguin Books India Pvt Ltd, 11 Community Centre, Panchsheel Park, New Delhi – 110 017,
India ▪ Penguin Group (NZ), 67 Apollo Drive, Rosedale, North Shore 0632, New Zealand
(a division of Pearson New Zealand Ltd) ▪ Penguin Books (South Africa) (Pty) Ltd,
24 Sturdee Avenue, Rosebank, Johannesburg 2196, South Africa

Penguin Books Ltd, Registered Offices:
80 Strand, London WC2R 0RL, England

First published in 2009 by Portfolio, a member of Penguin Group (USA) Inc.

1   3   5   7   9   10   8   6   4   2

Copyright © Sasha Abramsky, 2009
All rights reserved

LIBRARY OF CONGRESS CATALOGING IN PUBLICATION DATA
Abramsky, Sasha.
Inside Obama's brain / Sasha Abramsky.
p.   cm.
Includes bibliographical references and index.
ISBN 978-1-59184-302-3
1. Obama, Barack—Psychology.   2. Obama, Barack—Political and social
views.   3. Presidents—United States—Biography.   I. Title.
E908.3.A26 2009
973.932092—dc22   2009030610
[B]

Printed in the United States of America
Set in Vendetta with Gotham
Designed by Daniel Lagin

To Sofia and Leo

May every good dream come true.

CONTENTS

INSIDE
OBAMA'S
BRAIN

INTRODUCTION

SETTING THE STAGE

On a cold, windy, winter's day, Barack Obama looked down from his podium at the base of the Lincoln Memorial and surveyed the crowd. Even by Obama-mania standards, it was enormous. Hundreds of thousands of people were packed into the open spaces of the National Mall. They had traveled from all across the United States to be in the nation's capital. Many had journeyed from overseas. They had come, bundled up against the chill, to watch, and to listen to, history unfold.

This gathering, a star-studded musical extravaganza on the last Sunday of George W. Bush's presidency, was a prelude. Two days later Obama was going to be inaugurated as the country's forty-fourth president. Standing directly in front of the great stone statue of a seated Abraham Lincoln, three flags planted on either side of him, Obama, as he had done so many times during the election campaign, let his words soar skyward. "As I prepare to assume the presidency," he declared, his tone deep and sonorous, "yours are the voices I will take with me every day I walk into that Oval Office—the voices of men and women who have different stories but hold common hopes; who ask only for what was promised us as Americans—that we might make of our lives what we will and see our children climb higher than we did. It is this thread that binds us together in common effort; that runs through every memorial on this mall; that connects us to all those who struggled and sacrificed and stood here before."

Washington's monuments loom large in American pageantry. They bring the past to life, or rather our visions of the past. Thus was inauguration organizer Emmett Beliveau's decision to go beyond mere parades and brass bands and to put together a top-talent concert at the Lincoln Memorial two days before the swearing-in ceremony intended as a conscious nod to a noble heritage. It was designed to signify renewal—or, if you think more in marketing terms, a rebranding—of America; a reclaiming of destiny; a sense of the American ideal, contained within the original founding documents, finally within reach of being realized. It was meant to summon the ghosts of generations past to this new cause. Abolitionists. Suffragettes. Nineteen-thirties trade unionists. Second World War GIs. Civil rights protesters.

The concert was supposed to redefine who and what constituted America, from the opening piece, Aaron Copland's majestic "Lincoln Portrait," through to the finale, eighty-nine-year-old Pete Seeger, backed by Bruce Springsteen, singing the full-length, infused-with-radicalism version of "This Land Is Your Land." There was the imagery, projected on huge screens above the podium and along the mall, and reproduced on millions of television screens around the world, of ordinary workers doing their jobs throughout the land. There was the visual tribute to the African American singer Marian Anderson, denied permission to sing in Washington in the late 1930s by the Daughters of the American Revolution, brought to perform on the Mall afterward at the invitation of First Lady Eleanor Roosevelt. *The America of the recent past,* the program might have read, *the country that lavished wealth and attention on the few while neglecting the needs and stories of the many, is being ushered out today. Welcome to the unveiling of a new-model America. Welcome to a new beginning.*

Something transformative had occurred in the national conversation through the long primary campaign and then the presidential election season leading up to November 4, through the long weeks preceding the inauguration, and then during the inauguration festivities themselves. Catalyzed by the person and words of Obama, America, collectively, engaged in a discourse, around race and around identity, around national visions of progress and community, that has likely forever altered the country's own self-image as well as the image of the United States seen by the rest of the world. The Sunday after the election, *New York Times* journalist Michael Sokolove, reporting on Levittown, Pennsylvania, voters' overwhelming support for Obama, wrote that "the nation was transformed on Tuesday but what had to occur first was the transformation of individual voters."[1]

Over a period of months, millions of those voters had

confronted their own prejudices, their own sets of expectations as to what a "real" American was; and, come Election Day, they decided they could, after all, vote for a black man who had built a political career out of listening to ordinary people tell the stories of their lives. The excitement of crowds not just in America but around the world that night was, at least in part, an excitement born of the realization that what it meant to be an American had forever changed.

Such moments occur rarely in a nation's history. And when they do, the people behind them inevitably become the focus of our intense attention. While we might not want to literally explore the contours of Barack Obama's brain, we do very much, as a culture, want to understand how that brain works, what passions animate the forty-fourth president, what ideas and which individuals inhabit the mental recesses of this enigmatic figure. That's why Obama's every move is so obsessively scrutinized. *What sort of dog will he buy for his daughters? What kind of mental anguish did he go through before deciding to release the "torture memos" from the Bush era?* At the press conference commemorating his first one hundred days in office, an enterprising *New York Times* reporter even asked the president what experiences he had found "most enchanting" during his three-plus months as occupant of the White House.

In a very real way, we want answered the question "what makes Obama tick?" That core question is what *Inside Obama's Brain* sets out to answer. To do so, one has to ask a host of smaller questions: How does he approach problems? What ideas and intellectual theories make up his political credo? How does he communicate with friends and foes? How do his many skills play out in his chosen fields, the worlds of writing, organizing, law, and politics? And why is it that so many people not just in the United States but around the world are so seduced—and so willing to be seduced—by his words and his presence?

The responses, provided by relatives, friends, and colleagues from the many layers of Obama's extraordinary life, and by his own words—put forth in his books and essays, in media interviews spanning more than a decade, and in numerous campaign speeches and political meetings—reveal the complexity of a man who has become something of a mythical figure in his own lifetime.

In his place in the country's history, President Obama is, in many ways, a successor figure to Martin Luther King Jr. and his vision of a beloved community moving America away from its divided, segregated past; he is the lead member of what *New Yorker* editor David Remnick and others have termed the Joshua Generation—the generation of highly educated, professionally employed African Americans provided not only with a sense of possibility by those who came before (the so-called Moses Generation, who broke down the legal structures of segregation) but also with a powerful sense of mission and obligation.

To supporters and critics alike, Obama is seen as a once-in-a-lifetime charismatic leader. To his more extreme critics from the conservative fringe—die-hards convinced that he is a Manchurian candidate with a covert plan to undermine the American way of life—in seeking to claim the driver's seat within the Joshua Generation, Obama has shown himself to be a man of messianic pretensions with a naive following almost religious in its fervor. To at least some of his supporters, he exhibits the rare power to shift the tectonic plates of history through the sheer force of his will—without apparent irony, Oprah Winfrey introduced him to huge crowds as "the One." In an open letter to the victorious candidate written immediately after the election, the author Alice Walker wrote that he was "a balm for the weary warriors of hope, previously only sung about." His position as one of American history's most charismatic figures presents a great paradox, since for much of Obama's early career, he warned against community movements built around the magnetic presence of individuals. An overreliance on charisma, he believed, was ultimately why Chicago's first African American mayor, Harold Washington, a man whose photo hung on a wall of his office while he was a state senator, failed to create a movement capable of outliving him.

A messiah? A prophet? A redeemer? These are not labels to be worn—or rejected—lightly. Yet at least implicitly, however over-the-top such appellations are, they float around President Obama constantly.

And so in January 2009 Barack Obama arrived in the White House with almost impossibly high hopes surrounding him and his administration. In some ways, people expect of him what South Africans expected of Nelson Mandela in 1994: the ability to wave a wand and usher in a harmonious Golden Age. Behind Obama's campaign, behind his rhetoric, behind his election, there has always been both the burden and the promise of history; and it is a burden and promise that Obama himself is keenly aware of. "This is your victory," Obama told a huge crowd in Chicago's Grant Park minutes after the presidential race had been declared in his favor. Looking out on the crying, jubilant multitudes, with press reports flowing in from around the country of crowds spontaneously taking to the streets in cities large and small, it must have appeared to the president-elect as if he were watching America's own velvet revolution unfold in front of his eyes. "I know you didn't do this just to win an election, and I know you didn't do it for me. You did it because you understand the enormity of the task that lies ahead. For even as we celebrate tonight, we know the challenges that tomorrow will bring are the greatest of our lifetime—two wars, a planet in peril, the worst financial crisis in a century."[2]

Obama's can be no ordinary presidency. Simply by virtue of who he is, simply by virtue of the historical legacy carved by his campaign and his election, he has changed America and created the expectations for more changes—both institutional restructuring in the face of economic collapse and also psychological shifts in how America understands itself.

How will Obama use this extraordinary appetite for change to reshape the United States? *Inside Obama's Brain*, through exploring the basic motivating ideas, the central hopes and fears and dreams of America's forty-fourth president, chronicles the likely road ahead.

In many ways, Obama's moment is a business story almost as much as it is a striking political drama. Jerry Kellman, Obama's first and most influential mentor in the world of Chicago community organizing, always viewed the writings of management guru Peter Drucker as being as applicable to the world of organizing and of grassroots politics as to business. When he was training Obama, he oftentimes carried Drucker's books into their meetings. Drucker believed that successful modern corporations were horizontal organizations, with knowledge widely distributed throughout the workforce. It was a vision not too different from that the community organizers had of effective, democratic political structures. For Kellman, Drucker's words were revelations. "Who's your market? What's of value to them?" he would ask his young organizers. "Those are universal questions when you're trying to get a job done."[3]

By 2007–8, America as an entity, a giant corporation, to use a company analogy, was failing: Its workforce was deeply unhappy, and its management was dysfunctional—incapable of analyzing hard information dispassionately and without an ideological lens, unable to communicate effectively to its workers and with other corporations (countries). Candidate Obama's challenge was to convince a majority of shareholders—*voters*—that his management model was better; and in doing so, he presented lessons not just to the world of politics, but, almost as important, to the world of business. President Obama's every decision, at least in the early years of his administration, will take place against the backdrop of a business climate bleaker than any since the Great Depression.

In explaining how President Obama thinks and communicates, this is a book not simply for policy buffs but for anyone interested in group cultures, be they political or corporate. In an era in which distrust of the excesses of big business and the greed of many executives runs rampant, Obama's methods and his techniques for rebuilding bonds of trust between citizens and government will likely be studied by CEOs as avidly as by politics junkies.

Inside Obama's Brain is *not* a biography—many have been written; many more will be in the years ahead. This book is not among them. Nor is it a political history—the story of the campaign has already been told, the story of Obama's administration cannot properly be told until he has had more time to govern. Writing in the winter and early spring of 2009, my words would likely be horribly dated by the time they reach the bookstores six months later. Moreover, while Barack Obama now walks the halls of power, and does so with tremendous ease, he did not grow up surrounded by powerful people; nor did he spend most of his adult life in such settings. "Most of my good friends are not in politics and are not in the political world," Obama told *Newsweek* reporter Daren Briscoe in May 2008.[4] To understand Obama the man, rather than Obama the myth, I believe one has to step away from Washington, D.C., and talk to the men and women who knew him in his other environs: in Honolulu, Los Angeles, New York, Chicago, and Cambridge.

And so, rather than an inside-the-Beltway scoop, a series of filtered interviews with today's Masters of the Universe, my book is intended as a psychological profile writ large, a peeling back of the veneer, a look into the mind of a man who now sits atop the peak of power. The first seven chapters are more about the interior workings of his mind; the last three about his public political persona and the ways in which that persona has been molded over the decades by his unique set of experiences and expectations. My attempt is to understand his motivations and his methods and in so doing to help my readers grasp the significance of Barack Obama's election to the presidency during a moment of profound national crisis and the likely changes that election presages for America's broader sense of self.

While I have covered campaign rallies at which Obama has spoken, I have not met the president one-on-one. During the reporting for this book, I contacted both the Transitional Team Press Office and then, after the inauguration, the White House Press Office repeatedly, requesting interviews with Barack and Michelle Obama, with members of the president's extended family, and with senior staffers. While the requests were never turned down, they were never approved, either. They were instead put into limbo, housed in what I can only assume to be a file marked "irritating: to be dealt with at an indeterminate time in the future." Each time I phoned back or e-mailed, I was told the requests were being processed or that they had been shunted up the chain of command. My guess is the president's handlers hoped the project would simply go away.

I do not minimize this omission. And yet Obama's life is,

in many ways, so publicly accessible—he has written so much, spoken in so many places, been interviewed so extensively—that most of the questions I would have posed to him directly were answerable, even without my meeting Obama, through referencing the president's own words.

Obama has been writing and speaking his own legacy into the history books since he was a young man. Of all the public figures of his generation, he is clearly the master communicator. He has also proven himself to be its dominant political strategist, a young man who seized the opportunities that presented themselves and rode them, at great speed, to the White House. His presence and his accomplishments invite historical comparisons, some made by third-party observers, to Franklin Roosevelt, to John Kennedy—others, in particular the Lincoln comparison, consciously cultivated by Barack Obama himself.

The nation's forty-fourth president invokes Abraham Lincoln so frequently not because the sixteenth president was a pure idealist—for much of his career, as he explicitly declared in his first inaugural address, he was willing to preserve the institution of slavery if such preservation would peaceably keep intact the Union—but because Lincoln's words, often soaring in their delivery, and actions cumulatively paved the way for a new imagining of America's innate possibilities. However pragmatic Lincoln's initial motivations, history conspired to make him the Great Emancipator; and in so doing it made him the nineteenth century's greatest spokesman for the American Dream, the man whose stone image would stand sentinel over King as he uttered the words of his "I Have a Dream" speech in 1963 and over Barack Obama as he addressed the audience at his preinauguration concert on January 18, 2009.

In recent years, the American Dream had seemed increasingly beleaguered. The gap between rich and poor had grown to levels not seen since the 1920s; millions of families had either lost their homes to foreclosures or depleted their life savings in desperate bids to keep their properties as variable interest rates kicked in and home values plummeted; and international goodwill toward America, long taken as a given by the American public, had all but evaporated.

In the two-year saga of the primary season and presidential campaign, Barack Obama had to convince an increasingly battered people first, that the system wasn't so rigged as to be impervious to the popular will; and second, that enough people *should* feel empowered to actually change things that, collectively, their votes *could* actually change things and kick-start a moribund dream once more.

That's where his community organizing skills and the language of self-help he perfected in Chicago in the 1980s came in handy. "How do you include the excluded in this country?" Obama asked his audience at a roundtable on community organizing held in the Windy City in 1990. "How do you get people who are on the outside of the mainstream into the mainstream? And also, how do you get that mainstream to change through that process, to get rich and examine itself and remake itself?"[5]

These were questions the grand theorists of community organizing had been posing for decades. "Where do ordinary people . . . gain the courage, the self-confidence, and above all the hope to take action in their own behalf?" Harry Boyte, founder and codirector of the Center for Democracy and Citizenship at the University of Minnesota, and his wife, Sara Evans, a history professor at the university, asked in their 1986 book *Free Spaces: The Sources of Democratic Change in America*.[6] "What are the structures of support, the resources, and the experience that generate the capacity and the inspiration to challenge 'the way things are' and imagine a different world?" Free spaces, the authors declared, "are the environments in which people are able to learn a new self-respect, a deeper and more assertive group identity, public skills, and values of cooperation and civic virtue."[7]

For Obama in 2008, the challenge—and the opportunity— was to re-create the United States itself as a Free Space writ large. "People need to be involved in shaping their own destinies. You don't make change from inside the status quo," remarked Marshall Ganz, a Harvard University Kennedy School lecturer in public policy and longtime grassroots organizer, who would serve as head of the Obama campaign's Civic Engagement Subcommittee in 2008.[8] "You have to build a new constituency with which to make change." Doing so would involve not just an election win based around a series of smart strategies and a dose of old-fashioned luck, but a profound shift in the American psyche, in the understanding of what good governance and civic engagement could make possible.

The Yale University political scientist Stephen Skowronek, author of *Politics Presidents Make: Leadership from John Adams to Bill Clinton*, has a theory about the preconditions needed for transformative presidents to emerge. The awful and the great seem to come in pairs in American history, Skowronek believes. Quite simply, Obama couldn't have emerged had not George Bush's discredited presidency made the country willing to take a great leap into the unknown to get out of the morass left by the forty-third president and his team.

Transformative presidencies emerge out of the ashes of a previous method of governance, out of the collapse of a set of governing principles and dominant economic ideas. "A transformational president is one who comes to power at a time when what has been for many years if not decades the received commitments of ideology and the interests of the federal government have been indicted and bankrupted and failed," Skowronek argues.[9] Such men have always managed both to look forward and, in a nod to the disorganization and chaos of their moment, to cast a nostalgic glance backward to better days now gone, to mythic American values and first principles now threatened. "It's always a rediscovery of fundamental values."

Obama fits this mold. He is both a radical and, in some ways, a true conservative; he talks both of reaffirming America's original social compact—which, as a constitutional lawyer, he has studied in depth—and at the same time implementing sweeping changes to move the country into new territory both economically and socially.

The day after the election, I posted a piece on the *Huffington Post* in which I put forward my opinion that Obama's election had, in a sense, taken the country forward in time through a wormhole— bringing political events that we might have expected in the distant future within reach of the present—that it represented a huge leap in the way in which the country approached both race relations and policy discussion. Many people responded to my essay, but the words of one blogger, in particular, caught my attention. In declaring the election a moment that moved us forward in time, I had missed half of the story, my anonymous correspondent argued. The other half was that it had also taken us backward just over forty years, back to the months before Martin Luther King Jr. and Bobby Kennedy were killed. Imagine what America might have looked like, what it might have become, the writer suggested, if King had lived to push his vision not just in the South but across the country, if RFK had become president and had used the full force of the government to really tackle the country's social problems. Imagine if the last third of the American century and the first eight years of the next had not been dominated by endless culture wars, scandals, political bickering, and an economic philosophy that ended up beggaring tens of millions of hardworking Americans.

In a profound way, the presidential election result of November 4, 2008, began the job of repairing a ripped historical fabric. When Obama stresses the dignity of work or reaches back to Lincoln through symbolic gestures such as swearing the oath of office on the Bible sworn on by the nation's sixteenth president, he is asking his audience to imagine they live in a country once again defined by basic, salt-of-the-earth, core values. Those values might always have been more mythic than real, or at least more complex than we paint them today as having been; but, as Obama, a bestselling memoirist, understands all too well, sometimes the stories we tell about ourselves, the narratives we weave out of the raw material of our experiences, are as important as the actual realities we live. "History's a funny muse," explains Rice University and CBS News historian Douglas Brinkley. "People can go shopping for what they want."[10]

Sure, Lincoln, for much of his career, reluctantly accepted the institution of slavery. Sure, unlike Obama—who by all indications has a picture postcard family and near-seamless relationship with his wife, Michelle, and daughters, Malia and Sasha—Lincoln had a notoriously troubled personal life. Sure, Lincoln was emotionally unstable and prone to profound depressions, while Obama fashions himself as "No Drama Obama," but for all of that, the myth of a Lincoln resurrection, of a twenty-first-century reincarnation of the man who saved the Union, is too potent to willingly punch holes in. Thus while Obama, a keen student of history, is surely aware of the limits of the comparison, he also knows the value of that comparison and uses it to the full. "It is that fundamental belief, it is that fundamental belief—I am my brother's keeper, I am my sister's keeper—that makes this country work," Obama told his spellbound audience at the Democratic National Convention in Boston, on July 27, 2004. "It's what allows us to pursue our individual dreams, and yet still come together as one American family: 'E pluribus unum,' out of many, one."

For Obama's close friend and political confidant Cassandra Butts, Obama became during the election season something of a cultural Rorschach test.[11] People saw in him what they wanted to see in their broader community—they invested in his person hopes they had dared not even articulate in recent decades.

That's why, in his inauguration speech, when talking of the "gathering clouds and raging storms" of our era, Obama can call on people to serve, to sacrifice, and not be either ignored, like Bush, or despised as a mealy-mouthed naysayer, like Jimmy Carter. *Do so,* he tells his audience, *and I'll lead you, you'll lead yourself to better times ahead.* No B.S., no cajoling. *We're all adults,* he implies, *you can trust me because I'll give it to you as I see it.* In a less gifted communicator, this would lead to bitterness, to recrimination; with Obama it leads to a sense of national camaraderie. Even many of his political opponents end up wanting him to succeed.

In an era in which America seemed to have been brought low by political partisanship and growing economic and cultural divides, Obama promised unity. His polyglot identity and his boundlessly self-confident rhetoric seemed to offer a way out of the dead ends old-school politicians had driven the country into. His uncanny political instincts allowed voters to glimpse both lost glories and future glories, to imagine there were new chapters still to be written about the American Dream. Perhaps it was with that understanding in mind that Teddy Kennedy decided, early in the primary process, to cast his lot with Obama. *The Kennedy family,* the old senator reputedly told his son, Patrick, *had to be on the right side of history.*[12] He had a startling ability to empathize with the downtrodden—of whom there were ever more in the waning days of the Bush presidency—and to project calm amid chaos. Charlie Halpern, founder of the Center for Law and Social Policy and a celebrated book author, believed he was a true practitioner of what Halpern termed "wisdom." Through his memoirs and his other writings, Obama could pitch himself to a therapy-driven culture, Halpern believed, as the first "self-analyzed president."[13]

"What has found its way onto these pages," Obama wrote in the introduction to *Dreams from My Father,* "is a record of a personal, interior journey—a boy's search for his father, and through that search a workable meaning for his life as a black American."[14] Several years later, speaking at a New York City Barnes & Noble in late November 2004 as a then newly elected senator, Obama told his audience that he had written *Dreams from My Father* as a way to try to answer a fundamental question: "How do we expand a sense of empathy and allow each and every one of us to be able to stand in someone else's shoes and see the world through their eyes, and as a consequence see ourselves in other people?"[15]

Obama's relationship to the written and spoken word is central not just to his success as a politician, to his image as an empathetic leader, but to his very being. "Barack was a writer first and a politician second," says his media guru and adviser David Axelrod's partner, John Kupper,[16] one of the friends on whom Obama called to read drafts of *The Audacity of Hope* as he prepared the manuscript to send off to his publishers. Watch Obama sign his books after a book reading, and you are watching a man in his element, putting his terrific people skills to use as he sells his books and wins over his audiences: He talks with each person for only a few seconds, yet in those moments he establishes a rapport with them; he asks them their name, what they do, a couple other quick questions; he flashes his brilliant smile; and, with a rapid lefty flourish, he dashes off a signature. When there's a large crowd, he might have four or even five of these interactions in a minute. When the people at his readings respond positively to his words, he looks genuinely happy, the artist surveying his own exhibition opening.

Michelle Obama reputedly told friends that putting pen to paper was never a painful experience for her husband; rather, it was cathartic. The hours he would spend every day honing the words of his books or writing columns and opinion pieces for newspapers were hours in which he gave his soul free rein.

Shortly after the Obamas moved into the White House, aides began giving the president a purple folder every day, containing a selection of letters from ordinary Americans around the country, expressing their hopes and concerns. Obama, according to ABC News, would take the time to personally reply to two or three of these letters.[17] The letters would help him sharpen his ideas on the pressing issues of the moment. Perhaps, too, they made him feel more connected to his constituents; if security concerns meant that he could no longer go on long walks through the city whenever he felt like it, well at least he could still let his words wander through the crowds for him.

But who exactly is the man behind these words?

Inside Obama's Brain teases that person out. It explores the ideas that animate the country's forty-fourth president: the values behind his policies, the organizing ideals behind his political campaigns. And it also looks at unique qualities that make Obama's character so compelling, in particular his sense of presence, empathy, and charisma.

During the election campaign, the GOP mocked Barack Obama for being "only" a community organizer in his early career. Much of the media, including his biographers, have concluded that the community organizing period of Obama's life should be accorded relatively little space, assuming those years simply reflected the radical foibles of a young man trying to find himself.

What these commentators missed was that the beliefs that led Obama into community organizing a quarter century ago, along with the skills he perfected while an organizer, were both key to who he became politically and also made him the perfect candidate in an election dominated by fear, a sense of national malaise, and a desperate yearning for better times ahead. This book explores the central role the community organizing ethos occupies in Obama's character and details how that ethos made him, in a most out-of-the-ordinary election year, an extra-ordinarily versatile presidential candidate.

In the mid-1980s, Obama went through a series of "orga-nizing schools" in Chicago. At the Gamaliel Foundation and other locales, long-time organizers taught him hands-on techniques that allowed him to connect with, and cultivate the trust of, ordi-nary people. They also taught him how to empower people, how to motivate ordinary citizens to change their environments.

I have not given "community organizing" a separate chapter heading in this book. That is not because it is unimportant. To the contrary: it is a leitmotif running through the entire Obama story. It is ubiquitous as background to practically every chapter within this book.

Over the course of a quarter century, Barack Hussein Obama has gone from being an idealistic young community organizer to president of the United States. It is, by any definition, an extra-ordinary story. Halfway through that story, when Obama was in the state senate in Illinois, he played a weekly poker game with several colleagues. Now, as president, he is bringing all the skills learned as a community organizer, as a writer, a lawyer, and a politician to the highest-stakes game on earth.

The following pages show how President Barack Obama plays the hands he's been dealt. In understanding how he emerged, we can glimpse where he is heading; and in seeing the paths that Obama is mapping out, we can see where America, as a country, is likely to go.

CHAPTER ONE

FOCUS

Back in the mid-1980s, the young organizer Obama arranged a training session for several community activists from South Side Chicago, teaching them how to tell their stories, how to lobby officials for such causes as the removal of asbestos from public housing units and the creation of local job training programs, and how to engage other community members in discussions about their neighborhoods' problems. He found a hotel off the interstate, on the way to Lansing, Michigan, and booked its conference room. It was, the activists noted to their dismay, in the middle of nowhere. Money was tight, and for most of them, trips away from Chicago were a rare luxury. *Why would he choose such a dismal locale for their retreat?*

"He said, 'I want to keep you focused. We could have gone somewhere else, but you would have wanted to shop and go to restaurants. And I want you all focused,'" recalls one of the women, Loretta Augustine-Herron, an organizer and teacher who worked closely with Obama during these years.[1] "I never will forget that. 'But we're going to have a party on the last night,'" Herron recalls Obama telling them, somewhat shamefaced. "And we did. It wasn't a wingding do. But it was his interpretation of a party." She pauses and laughs at the memory. "As young as he was, he was very focused on what he was doing. And he researched everything. He seemed so relaxed, when he would be sitting there talking to us. But you know what, we knew he knew. It was almost like a gift. He seemed to know how things fit together, where everything fit in the scheme of things."

When the organizers arranged public meetings to discuss dilapidated housing stock or lack of job training opportunities, Obama would diligently prep his team and then stand at the back of the room, silently, arms folded, carefully listening to what was being said. He wouldn't look for the spotlight, but if things began to veer out of control, he'd step in, carefully, respectfully, and steer the conversation back on track.

"He came into our homes, went into the homes of those people in the projects. The older people just loved him to death," recalled another one of the community activists, Yvonne Lloyd, more than two decades later.[2] Lloyd was an elderly lady with eleven children, twenty-four grandchildren, and thirteen great-grandkids, living in Nashville, Tennessee, by the time her friend was elected president. For her, looking back across the years, the young Obama had had a simply magnetic quality. She noticed that people far older than Barack just wanted to follow him. "He'd tell us, 'if people around you are acting crazy, yellin' and hollerin', you all stay calm. Stay focused.' That was the way he trained us. That's the person I knew, that's the Barack I know. A young man who could lead a group of people in which everyone was much, much older than he was. I can remember, a lady said to me—she wasn't in our group—she said, '*girl*, you all follow that man?' I said, 'if you get to know him, if you're involved in community work, you *want* to follow him, because you *believe* he can get things done.' I felt like he was one of my children. I wanted him to succeed."

RATS, GOLF, AND THREE-POINT BASKETS

From the time he was very young, focus and the ability to filter out the surrounding white noise have been core facets of Barack Obama's personality. Perhaps it was a legacy of the middle-of-the-night English lessons his mother would make him sit through as a small boy in Indonesia. *Concentrate. Concentrate. Concentrate.* Friends from his days at the elite Punahou Academy, in Honolulu, recall that Barry, as he was then known, was always able to zoom in on individuals, to appear to give them his undivided attention. "He was very calm, very poised, a good listener as well as a good talker. Very eloquent," his homeroom teacher, Eric Kusunoki, known to the students simply as Mr. Kus, remembered.[3] "He was bright, articulate, had a good demeanor, got along well with everyone." Mr. Kusunoki and students from Obama's class recollected a happy, laid-back teenager, but one who knew how to focus intensely when he had to.

Throughout Obama's adult life, colleagues and friends have

been struck by this trait. When he sets a course, he is methodical in following through on it, never leaving tasks unfinished.

Chicago attorney Judson Miner, whose small civil rights law firm hired Obama out of Harvard—beating out several hundred other firms that were also wooing the one-time *Law Review* president, most of them corporate, many of them offering far larger salaries—came to believe that nothing would distract the young Obama.

Miner recalls a very specific example relating to his young colleague's ability to filter out even the most disgusting of distractions. Miner, Barnhill & Galland operated out of a house next to a small Thai restaurant. The restaurant had a problem with vermin—one that would ultimately result in its being closed down by the city—and the rats had begun venturing out into neighboring properties. One day, the attorneys were meeting en masse in the basement conference room. Obama took a call relating to a case he was working on. As he was speaking, two large rodents entered the conference room and started running around between the attorneys' legs. Stories have a habit of becoming larger in the telling, but law firm partner Chuck Barnhill swears that one of the creatures even climbed up Obama's leg. "And while we were all distracted by the rats," Miner says, laughing, "he focused on his conversation, finished his conversation, and then picked up on the conversation that we were having about the rats. He can juggle lots of things, and compartmentalize, so one thing doesn't interfere with another. He's very private in terms of things like that. He doesn't publicly declare either his anger or his grief or anything. But you know he's affected by things. You could tell by his facial expressions."[4]

"I remember Barack talking about it in his sort of wry way," says George Galland, who wasn't present at the infamous meeting.[5] "The context was 'what kind of a dump do you have me working in?!' We were being driven nuts by this family of rats." For Galland, the episode served as one of many examples of Obama's sangfroid. "He never gives you the impression of being distracted when he's talking to you. While he's talking to you, you do feel that you have his complete attention. And I suspect that you do. That's always been characteristic of him."

As far as Miner was concerned, this was a talent that couldn't be learned. It was, he felt, quite "natural." And it was also utterly compelling, instantly leaving an impression on anyone who met the young attorney. That same ability is what impressed Newton Minow, one of Chicago's top lawyers and a onetime chair of the Federal Communications Commission. He came in late to a gathering of the city's power brokers in the early 1990s, announced that he had been meeting with some young attorneys, Michelle and Barack Obama, and then declared, with great theatricality, that he had just seen the country's future.[6] Years later he would write an op-ed explaining why he hoped Obama would announce his candidacy for president. The senator knew how to cut to the chase; he knew how to zoom in on what was important and bring the broader public along with him. "He brings people together to find consensus," Minow wrote in a piece that ran in the

October 26, 2006, edition of the *Chicago Tribune*. "He is a different kind of political leader. He is a peacemaker."

That extreme focus, that drive to succeed at whatever he was doing, had marked Obama out from the crowd for as long as anyone could remember. As an adult, it was channeled into achieving political change. Earlier in his life, it was sometimes more about smaller, less socially meaningful triumphs. John Owens (referred to simply as Johnnie in *Dreams from My Father*), the man who replaced Obama as head of the Developing Communities Project when the community organizer went east to Harvard Law School, experienced his younger friend's need to succeed when they both were flown out to Los Angeles in the summer of 1986 to take part in a two-week-long training camp run by a community organizing school known as the Industrial Areas Foundation. Obama, who had grown up in Hawaii, regularly swimming in the Pacific Ocean, made it clear to Owens that he could, and *would*, outswim him in the waters off the Malibu coast. "I couldn't keep up with him swimming. This guy was extremely athletic. He's extremely competitive, man. I certainly wasn't up to his par in terms of swimming, and he wasn't going to take it easy on me. He said, 'Well, John, I won't suggest that you swim out with me. I see how you swim and I'm not going to help you back.' That kind of thing."[7] When they hit the tennis courts, Owens's boss played with a similar ruthlessness. This was the same Obama who, according to his half sister Maya, would whoop unceremoniously whenever he won at childhood games of Scrabble.[8]

Even on a golf course, Obama took victory seriously—though he wasn't actually that good at golf; he had a jerky, quarter-swing windup, which he repeated several times before striking the ball, and needed around ninety shots to complete an eighteen hole course. Nevertheless, recalls his friend Whitman Soule,[9] a data consultant who worked for Miner, Barnhill & Galland, he would want to spice up the games, played on public courses in Hyde Park and in the northern suburbs, by betting quarters on each hole; it wasn't exactly real money, but the mere fact of the bet seemed to get Obama's juices flowing. "It sort of added a . . . " Soule paused, thinking through the image. "This was not really competitive, but it *was* sorta mock-competitive. He enjoyed the additional dimension of it being competitive."

After the game ended, Obama would reach into his pocket and light up a cigarette. Then, if he didn't feel he had to go home to see Michelle or to do more work, the golf buddies would head over to Hackney's restaurant to eat and talk.

On an indoor tennis court, too, during Thursday afternoon and weekend games with Judson Miner at the East Bank or Lake Shore clubs, baseliner Barack would always play to win. Very focused, very methodical. A man with a tidy desk at the office and a no-nonsense attitude at the gym or on the tennis court. Each day, says fitness trainer Ruben Wilson, he would do the same three sets of bench presses and barbells. In between sets, he would read either the *Wall Street Journal* or, less often, the sports pages of *USA Today*. Obama was, according to Wilson and other gym regulars, only an average pickup basketball player, but if he got into the zone and started making shots, then you could expect him to make several great baskets in a row—he was focusing so hard on the game that he would actually start temporarily playing like a better player than he generally was. His focus shifted him up several gears.[10] *Sports Illustrated* journalist Alexander Wolff, who took to the basketball court with the candidate one day during the presidential campaign, reported that Obama was comfortable with throwing behind-the-back passes and nailed a surprising number of three pointers.[11]

Both John Owens and Judson Miner recognized that Obama's competitive nature when it came to sports represented something deeper than a mere outlet for a large ego. Winning mattered not only because Obama viscerally hated losing but because it vindicated his broader life strategy: stay focused on your goals, don't get distracted by the little things. Keep your life ordered, show determination, and things will start to break your way. Owens remembers Obama eating the same breakfast almost every day while at the Malibu retreat: eggs, hash browns, and toast, almost never with any meat thrown in—"he never ate to excess, everything was always in moderation"—and then spending hours exercising, either jogging in the hills or swimming in the ocean. He was disciplined, almost regimented in his personal behavior. Loretta Augustine-Herron remembered that many of the women in the Developing Communities Project would worry about his eating habits; at times, as he toured the area talking with unemployed steel workers, he seemed skinny to the point of near emaciation. One time, she recalled, Obama took them all out to lunch; and while they were eating club sandwiches and burgers, he nibbled on a spinach salad. "We were like, 'Barack, aren't you going to eat something? You know, that's *nothing*.' He told us he would get something later on; don't worry about it . . . that food slowed him down. It kept him from thinking clearly."[12] Nearly a quarter century later, reporters covering Obama's presidential campaign observed the same thing. While he sometimes barbecued for his kids at his home in Chicago, he himself rarely ordered red meat when out on the vote-gathering trail—preferring salmon instead, or a salad; he ate little at the many greasy-spoon diners he stopped to campaign in (he would purchase takeout pancakes in some restaurants, so as not to hurt the proprietors' feelings, but no one saw him eating the pancakes afterward); and he preferred to exercise alone rather than to small-talk with reporters and campaign volunteers over a few beers after a hard day of campaigning.[13]

While Obama was not bombastic, neither was he shy about flaunting his competitive nature. Owens recalls his boss taking offense when he teased him that he couldn't dance—and going out of his way, with mixed success, to try to prove him wrong at the R&B concerts and parties they occasionally went to together. Longtime friend William McNary, of the public interest group Citizen Action, remembers the time that Obama was invited onto a popular local radio show on which the host, Herb Kent the Cool Gent, and a guest would square off, convincing callers to back one or another music star in a popularity contest. Obama had to convince listeners to phone in to support Sam Cook's music over that of Lou Rawls. He took the task to heart as if his very future depended on it, and by the end of the show, he had racked up more calls than Herb Kent.

That sense of competitiveness was very much in line with his broader ambitions. Obama wanted to aim for the top, and he had the confidence to believe he could outcompete anyone he ran up against on the way. What did he think about maybe one day running for the presidency? *New York Times* columnist Bob Herbert asked Obama, less than two years after he had been elected to the U.S. Senate. "If you go into public service you want to have influence," the senator replied. "Obviously, the president has *the* most influence."[14] His self-confidence brings to mind the young John Kennedy's line "Sure it's a big job; but I don't know anyone who can do it better than I can."

Over the years, some have described this will to win as arrogant, in-your-face, or unpleasantly ambitious. For Toni Preckwinkle, a longtime Southside Chicago alderman, it appeared at times as if the young, upstart politician would tread on anyone and everyone's toes if it got him up that greasy pole to power. An Obama delegate to the Democratic National Convention in 2008, she nevertheless remained somewhat suspicious of his motivations. "He's a very smart and talented person," the alderman acknowledged, choosing her words carefully. "He has been extremely focused and single-minded as he's moved up the political ladder and had what I can only describe as a meteoric rise. He put together a very disciplined campaign staff to run for president, and they ran a brilliant campaign." *Did she like what Obama had done with his brilliance over the years?* The alderman paused, a long, pregnant pause, and then laughed nervously. "I don't think it matters whether I like it or not. He's been extraordinarily successful in the way he's chosen to operate. So that speaks for itself."[15]

Some of his university classmates have been quoted in news articles referring to his overblown ambitions, his arrogant certainty of his destiny. Some of his Democratic colleagues in the Illinois state senate were similarly unenthusiastic. And there were those in the world of progressive foundations that Obama frequented in the 1990s who came to feel that he used people and institutions to achieve his goals and then moved on.

Yet these men and women are the exceptions. Most of those who have come into contact with Obama over the years are struck by his quiet determination and focus rather than any fundamental sense of bluster.

During Obama's early days in Chicago, he was, according to several community organizers who worked closely with him in the South Side, obsessively immersed in reading. His apartment had no television and, while he was still feeling his way into his adopted city socially, he rarely went out evenings. They describe him at this point during his life as "monkish," utterly preoccupied with imbibing ideas. It was a habit he had brought with him from New York, from his years studying politics at Columbia University. "I spent a lot of time in the library," Obama told a student journalist from *Columbia College Today* in 2005. "I didn't socialize that much. I was like a monk." In Chicago, his mentors gave him books such as Robert Caro's *The Power Broker*, the classic text on New York City planner Robert Moses and the community organizing backlash his grandiose plans inspired; writings such as *Rules for Radicals*, by legendary organizer Saul Alinsky; and Bernard Crick's *In Defense of Politics*. He inhaled them as if they were oxygen rather than merely written words. He was, said his boss, Jerry Kellman, a young man of striking "discipline."[16]

Perhaps this was a subconscious reaction to the saga of his father. The elder Barack Obama was a brilliant but undisciplined man, prone to sabotaging both his happiness and his career through fits of anger, womanizing, drinking to excess, mocking his bosses and colleagues, and abandoning one wife after another and one set of children after the next. If Bill Clinton was the needy, attention-grabbing, physical affection–craving son of an abusive alcoholic, Obama was the cerebral, focused son of a skittish, high-strung dilettante, an Ivy League–educated economist who could have ended up in the highest echelons of power in Kenya but instead finished his life a broken, frustrated might-have-been.

But Obama wasn't just monkish. Even in his early twenties, he was seen as being extremely methodical, a skill not always in evidence in the prickly, ego-clashing world of community organizing and grassroots politics. Too often, community organizers would get frustrated and wouldn't finish what they set out to do. Too often alliances would break down in the face of personality conflicts. For Obama, this was never an issue. "Why organize?" he titled his contribution to the volume of essays edited by Peg Knoepfle and published in 1990 under the title *After Alinsky*.[17] "Probably the shortest [answer] is this: It needs to be done, and not enough folks are doing it." Concentrate on community organizing, he wrote, and you can generate a "surge of political empowerment around the country." Listen and learn. Bring people on board. Make them feel important. Give them your undivided attention.

When the organizers were campaigning to get the Chicago Housing Authority to remove asbestos from the Altgeld Gardens housing projects, Obama could often be found at the CHA offices, trawling through files for information, looking for the names of obscure officials to talk with.[18] Afterward, in church-basement meetings around the South Side, he'd parcel out the information among the organizers. He'd sometimes show up at seven thirty AM meetings, remembered Loretta Augustine-Herron, and keep going to meetings and talking with people until after ten o'clock at night.

"He was very interested in people, very empathetic," said the Gamaliel Foundation's Mike Kruglik. "He later said that the fundamental concepts of community organizing were seared into his brain. One of those was the importance of listening to people, and finding out their story, their passion, and their core motivation, their self-interest."[19] For Harry Boyte, this was not just a technique; it was the inculcation of a new sensibility. "Broad-based organizing," he believed, "tried to create countercultures to a broader culture it thought was debased, materialist. That would have been a very formative experience for Obama."[20]

Later on, in the months between graduating from Harvard and starting work at Miner's law firm, Obama ran Project Vote, hired by the project's funder, attorney Sanford Newman, at a salary that translated to less than $30,000 per year.[21]

Once again, he focused on the task at hand as if his very life depended on it. In a half-year period, the campaign—using its own volunteers and specially trained workers from already-existing local organizations—registered well over 150,000 new voters, far more than any other single voter registration drive in Illinois history. Obama kept week-by-week registration tallies and carefully calculated how many volunteers were needed at each registration site. The vast majority of these new voters were African American, in a city in which black citizens, following Mayor Harold Washington's death, had opted out of the political process in alarmingly high numbers. By the end of the 1992 election campaign, Obama's team, effectively using the slogan "It's a Power Thing," had engineered a remarkable transformation: For the first time ever, the number of registered voters in Chicago's nineteen mainly black wards outnumbered the numbers registered in the city's mainly white wards.[22]

Somehow, at the same time as he was working flat-out on Project Vote—Newman thought he was putting about seventy hours a week into it—Obama managed to pen most of his book *Dreams from My Father*. Friends theorized that he slept only three or four hours a night.

It was a pattern that would repeat itself time and again over the next decade. Obama always did many things at once: he was a lawyer at Miner's firm; he was a lecturer—and then a senior lecturer—at the University of Chicago law school; he was a state senator; and he was an author. And yet he seemed to always manage to stay on top of things; friends recall that they would e-mail him and get responses not days later but within a few minutes.

During the editing process for *The Audacity of Hope*, Obama was traveling in Africa. Unable to access fax and e-mail links and with a tight publishing schedule leaving no margin for error, he phoned his editor repeatedly, from Djibouti, Chad, and Kenya, to go over the line edits. One call went through the entire night, a five-hour marathon session with not a single break. Obama's concentration never wavered. He wanted to make sure every word was just so. This wasn't the editing style of a politician dashing out a campaign book simply for name recognition; rather, it was the style of a committed writer laying bare his mind for the world to see and wanting that mind to come across as a polished, stylish instrument.

His work, Crown Publishing editor Klayman found, needed hardly any line editing. When he wrote a passage, he would keep revisiting it, worrying away at the text to get it just right. Klayman, who had been an editor for nearly a quarter century, believed Obama the writer was a true perfectionist. "If you're the teacher filling in the bubble for the reference, he's in the top one percent," she felt. Over the years, she had encountered only three or four other writers whose copy was so clean.[23]

TUNING OUT DISTRACTIONS

During Obama's run for the U.S. Senate, the *Chicago Sun-Times* quoted a friend from his Harvard Law School days saying their mutual hero while they were students was Michael Jordan, a basketball superstar who combined talent with a passion for competition and a preternatural ability to focus on the job at hand. On court, recalls law school professor Alan Dershowitz, who used to play ball with Obama, he'd excel with a devastating lefty jump shot. "He was just good at everything. Everybody liked him. He was the kind of guy, you looked at him and said to yourself, 'he's going somewhere.'"

Out of approximately 550 law school students who pass through Harvard each year—students being groomed to assume elite positions within American society—Dershowitz says that he feels this way about perhaps a dozen. Of these dozen, he's right about half the time: These are the men and women who end up going on to become senators, governors, top trial lawyers, Supreme Court justices, and, yes, presidents.[24]

Even Obama's critics—and in the early days in Springfield, there were many of them, several of whom were dime-a-dozen figures from within his own party, knocked off stride by the newbie's poise—swiftly recognized his prodigious intellectual and political talents. They saw as well his ability to home in on issues and bring disparate groups and individuals together to support his goals.

As he has moved up the political ladder, that focus has stayed with him. "Here's another little example," says Colorado-based pollster Paul Harstad. "This is the summer of 2004. He had the Democratic nomination for the senate. It's approximately June, might have been July. For a while, he didn't have an opponent. We didn't know if it would be a strong candidate or a weak candidate.

But anyway, he wants to hold an issues meeting. He was doing his job as state senator. And he took that job very seriously. So he wanted to hold an issues meeting in Springfield. They drove down about twenty advisers. There were some issues advisers, top campaign staff and consultants. They're trying to find new innovative, progressive, enlightening approaches to education, health care, the economy, and approaches to foreign policy." The meeting lasted more than five hours. "Barack himself would start on the issues and of all the ideas offered up, he offered up eighty-five to ninety percent of them. He had the issues nailed. He's eager to hear things—he likes to hear new information, new approaches, new ideas—but he's just got the issues mastered. There was basically no politics in the meeting. There was almost no mention of politics. It was solid substance, policy. It was remarkable in the middle of a campaign to have it so purely substantive, merit-based, without real regard to political consideration."[25]

Yet for all his emphasis on focus and accomplishment, Obama isn't a micromanager—indeed, those close to him say he chooses top talent to surround him and then delegates well in the confidence that his team will present him with good information and policy choices. "The brilliance of his campaign is, he put together a small team of brilliant people, and then he got out of the way. I've seen a lot of campaigns," said Alan Solomont, the first big Bill Clinton financier to publicly back Obama. "And I've never seen a candidate who was less of a micromanager. He clearly was part of setting strategy. He said 'I want to run it like a business. I want it to show respect. And I want no drama.' He put together Axelrod and Plouffe, Gibbs and Hildebrand, and what have you, not a big group, and he really then let them run things. I've never seen a campaign where there weren't people coming and going. None of that in this campaign."[26]

"Barack likes the big picture. He has little patience for implementation of detail," asserts his friend Ken Rolling, who first met Obama in the mid-1980s and later worked alongside him at the Annenberg Challenge. When he needed to master minutiae, he was more than capable of doing so. But he preferred to work on a huge canvas, looking to make connections between ideas and policies too often sealed off from each other by bureaucracies and specialty interests. By inclination, his responses to policy problems were holistic. Obama wanted to know the broad contours of the research experts were compiling; but he didn't feel that as chairman he was personally responsible for all of the tiny details being set in motion. "He wants to know what the strategy is his staff will carry out. He wants to be able to set the direction and have good people stepping up to implement the details."[27]

Combining self-confidence with trust in his team, Obama presents to observers a striking sense of inner calm. Many people, including senior leaders of his presidential transitional team, describe it as almost Zen-like. In the same way as he tunes out distractions while on the basketball court, when he's in the political zone, nothing seems to bother him. It is a modus operandi diametrically opposed to, say, that of Bill Clinton or Richard Nixon, both of whom were very smart and cognizant of the big picture and their role in history, but neither of whom could get entirely past the little distractions.

In the early fall of 2008, as the American economy teetered on the edge of an abyss and one financial institution after another simply crumbled to dust, that ability to home in on the issues allowed Obama to emerge as the most intellectually serious presidential candidate. With voters suddenly looking for substance, Obama had no problem portraying the necessary gravitas, convincing experts and ordinary citizens alike that, despite his youth, he knew what he was about. Advisers recall him convening a meeting with Warren Buffett and several other top financial experts at the height of the crisis. In a room of economic all-stars, Obama quickly sized up the issues and respectfully but firmly took control of the conversation.[28]

That focus guided Obama through the remaining months of the marathon presidential contest. On November 3, 2008, the day before the election, Obama stumped in Jacksonville, Florida. "The time for change has come. We have a righteous wind at our backs," he told the enthused crowd. It sounded poetic. It also sounded like the words of a man with his eyes utterly trained on the prize, convinced that he was surfing the waves of destiny.

CHAPTER TWO

LOOKING INWARD, REACHING OUTWARD

Obama often says that the core values of his mother, Stanley Ann, shaped who he was and what he believed in. She was, he wrote in the preface to the 2004 edition of *Dreams from My Father*, "the kindest, most generous spirit I have ever known,"[1] a woman who "gathered friends from high and low, took long walks, stared at the moon, and foraged through the local markets of Delhi or Marrakesh for some trifle."[2]

Stanley Ann's mother, the woman Obama knew as Toot, called her daughter "an Adlai Stevenson liberal"—someone earnest in her love of the liberalism of the New Deal years, convinced that ideas really do matter, adamantly opposed to the infringements of civil liberties that McCarthyism had unleashed, and dedicated to bringing about an end to racial discrimination within the United States; and generally in writings about her that description has sufficed. After all, while Obama is eloquent in his protestations of filial love for his mother, he actually writes about her far more sparingly than he does many other important people in his life. In his public utterances, she remains something of an enigma, a remarkable lady, a globe-trotter, a crusader for social justice and "position-paper liberalism," but someone whose voice never is brought to the fore by her talented son. She is, in his writings, a silhouette. Read *Dreams from My Father*, and you're left with a far stronger impression of the individual, idiosyncratic traits of Obama's grandparents, even of some of his grandfather's friends, than you are of Stanley Ann Dunham. Subsequently, after her death, friends posit that he simply found it too painful to write about her, or to talk about her, publicly. And so the image fallen back on is of the Stevenson liberal.

In many ways, though, that seems an impression too rooted in the 1950s, when Obama's mother was still a young girl, to do justice to the adult Stanley Ann. It might have been the impression that Toot, herself a woman of the New Deal years, *wanted* her daughter to make on people, but it doesn't come off as a genuinely three-dimensional portrait of a complex young woman who bore a mixed-race son while still a teenager, divorced in her early twenties, remarried and moved halfway around the world in her mid-twenties, accumulated high academic honors, and, throughout her life, refused to compromise with the conventions of her era.

Photos of Stanley Ann suggest she was something of a flower child or, at the very least, a Beat poetess. She was, said friends, a free spirit, a wanderer. For her daughter, Maya, she was someone who exuded a sense of "humanity. She was brave enough to see people for the best that resided in them, to never assume that there was a person out there who was impenetrable, who she couldn't impact in some way or touch in some way. That was really heroic." Wherever she went, whomever she spent time with, said Maya, she managed to create loyal communities of friends, "people who were like-minded, who loved her, and would laugh with her."[3] It was, she believed, a character trait inherited by her brother, Barack.

During a period in which interracial marriages were rare—radical political statements in and of themselves—and generally considered to be the legitimate target of everything from malicious gossip to physical violence, Stanley Ann married first a Kenyan student and then an Indonesian. She had a son by the Kenyan and a daughter by the Indonesian and encouraged her children to be proud of their heritage and wide-ranging in their worldviews. She was, a thirty-four-year-old Obama told interviewer Connie Martinson in an interview at her studio in Los Angeles in the summer of 1995 during his book tour for *Dreams from My Father*, a "proponent of Afro-centric education before it became fashionable. Because she really emphasized and built up a strong self-image for me of what it meant to be an African and an African American. That I should be proud of that heritage and that culture."[4] As an anthropologist—her PhD dissertation focused on Javanese blacksmiths who used scrap metal to make farm and kitchen tools—she lived overseas for years, not within the affluent confines of the American diplomatic and business community but as an adoptive Indonesian.[5] And, as someone with expertise in microlending, she was more at home working with the rural poor than hobnobbing with fellow expats in expensive Western enclaves. She liked jazz music, was spiritual although not in any conventional sense religious, and enjoyed discussing politics with her university friends.

Stanley Ann took Barack with her to Indonesia in 1967, the year of the Summer of Love and a period during which hippies were embarking on journeys of self-discovery from Morocco to India. A few years later, she sent her son back to Hawaii. She and Barack's half sister, Maya, stayed in Indonesia just long enough for her marriage to collapse. And then she, too, returned to Hawaii. Yet she remained peripatetic. For much of Obama's pre-teen and teenage years, she was traveling, with Maya in tow—and during those times, Obama would live with Stanley Ann's parents. Indeed, from the time he was sixteen until he was twenty, Barack's mother lived in Indonesia, and they would see each other only on Christmas trips and during the summers.

Obama was a half-black, half-white teenager, with a half-white, half-Asian sister living thousands of miles away with his mother among rural Javanese craftsmen,[6] and an array of half siblings in Kenya whom he had never met. Some of his ancestors were Christians, some Muslim, others animists. He lived in a small apartment with his grandparents from Kansas, in a Hawaii mainly populated by whites, Japanese Americans, and indigenous Hawaiians.

Of all the states in the union, Hawaii, during the time Obama was being raised there, was the most polyglot. It was a majority nonwhite state; it was young enough to not be bedeviled by the same racial schisms that plagued the rest of the country in the

1960s and 1970s; and, thousands of miles from the mainland, it had developed a culture that, while identifiably American, was also quite distinct. Whether you were white or brown or black, if you lived on the islands, you were first and foremost a Hawaiian. And yet, even by Hawaii's standards, Obama's story was unusual.

Not surprisingly, Stanley Ann's son defied easy categorization.

"I GOT THE NAME FROM AFRICA AND THE ACCENT FROM MY MOTHER"

If *Dreams from My Father* can be read as an accurate window into the author's soul as a teenager and young adult, Obama struggled mightily with identity issues, running the gamut in his responses to his own complex history from confusion and self-destructiveness to anger, bravado, and pride. He went from being known as Barry to answering to his birth name, Barack, meaning "blessed one" in Arabic and Swahili. (His sister, Maya, the only person still alive to have shared a home with him during his childhood, rolls the "r" in his name, and overly stresses the second syllable. Listen to her discussing her brother in interviews and his name sounds something like "BarrrACK.") He grew an Afro. He started reading books and essays by Malcolm X. He attempted to reconcile himself with his father's absence, and then, in 1982, his death in a car accident in Kenya—a process that involved a careful demythologizing of Barack Sr., whom Stanley Ann, in his absence, had built up to be a man of almost royal stature. The young man also came to understand that no matter how much his mother and grandparents loved him, at some point he would need to figure out his identity by himself and on his own terms.

A few years later, when he met the Reverend Alvin Love in his South Side Chicago Lilydale First Baptist church, he could sense that the churchman was somewhat confused as to who he was and what he represented. After all, he didn't *sound* like he was from the neighborhood. "He felt some reticence on my part when he first came to my church to visit me," Love recollected. "He came in and he said 'my name is Obama.' He knew the first thing in my mind would be 'What about that last name? Am I dealing with a Muslim? Who is this guy and what's he selling?' He says to me, 'So, you're wondering where I got this funny accent from.' Which throws the question in a different direction. He says, 'My mother's from Kansas and my dad's from Kenya. I got the name from Africa and the accent from my mother.' He joked about it. He took that reticence right out. And you feel free to just go ahead and talk."

By his late teens and early twenties, as a student at Occidental College, in Los Angeles, and then at New York's Columbia University, Barack Obama had managed to carve out a coherent self-image as an American black man, albeit one with life experiences dramatically different from those of most of his peers. As he matured into adulthood, he chose to live in Chicago's predominantly black South Side rather than, say, Lincoln Park or North Shore; he married an African American woman; and he surrounded himself with a coterie of close friends—Valerie Jarrett, John Rogers, Marty Nesbitt, and others—who all were products of the South Side. Many of them would later be dispatched around the country during the early days of the 2008 presidential campaign to convince skeptical African American leaders that he really was "black enough" and also that he had the ability to bring blacks and whites alike into a new winning electoral coalition.

The reader of *Dreams from My Father* comes away with the sense of a profound anger welling up within the teenage and young-adult Obama as he struggles to make sense of who he is, but one that rapidly dissipates as he channels his talents into working for social change. Long before he applies to Harvard Law School, anger is replaced by something more constructive, by an understanding that the past never entirely determines the present and future, that there is always room to grow among the shadows cast by history. And as that understanding grows, so Obama's unquenchable sense of hope starts to blossom.

Because Obama's background is so hard to categorize, because his identity doesn't lend itself to pigeonholing, over the years he has become a synthesizing figure. He is part white, part black, part rooted in Kansas, part in Kenya. He grew up in Indonesia and also Hawaii. He is familiar with the Muslim culture of Indonesia, itself heavily influenced by Buddhism as well as Hindu beliefs from the Indian subcontinent, but is a member of a black Christian church in Chicago. He is an urbanite who while living in Indonesia owned a pet ape given to him by a stepfather who had seen jungle warfare while serving in his country's army. He is an all-around metropolitan man with Kenyan relatives and half siblings living in small rural villages and communities, which he journeyed to both as a young adult and, twenty years later, as a feted U.S. senator, a favorite son returning to his ancestral homeland.

There's something almost mythological to this story, something that, as he noted repeatedly in his stump speeches throughout 2008, is deeply improbable. His very existence challenges social codes and prevailing orthodoxies. Obama is, in many ways, a walking one-man diaspora, a man who can't be defined, or rather *confined*, by his many heritages, but who instead has to weave those heritages—threads that generally do not come together—into a coherent narrative of identity. To a peculiar degree, he is, as a result, his own creation.

The tangled, sprawling roots upon which rest Barack Obama's unconventional story almost force him into a sense of empathy, or understanding, with the rest of the world. He is, after all, not just the embodiment of *biracial*, but also of *multicultural*—not in the pejorative use of the word, implying that he lacks a core or is a grab bag of different cultural themes, but in a more profound sense: that he really *is* a person whose roots and references defy easy categorization and limitation, that his origins create the possibility of transcending cultural barriers. In his book *Kinship: A Family's Journey in Africa and America*, Philippe Wamba, himself the progeny of an African American woman and a Congolese man who had met at an American university in the 1960s, wrote that "although balancing two cultures within the same family sometimes involved shifting identities in shifting contexts, in some ways my family managed to situate itself on the boundary between cultural and continental communities." Wamba, who attended Harvard as an undergraduate at the same time that Obama was at the law school, found that "in the joining of two families, cultures, and nations that my parents represented, my brothers and I were bestowed a heritage rooted in both Africa and America."[7] Obama's story represented a similar balancing act.

CREATING A COMMUNITY TO CALL ONE'S HOME

The historian Douglas Brinkley posits that the early twentieth-century president Teddy Roosevelt viewed the American West as a physical space in which to heal the post–Civil War North/South divide. His writings about the West, published before he won the presidency, were intended to create an appropriate mythology within which national healing could occur. Sure, two large parts of the country had recently engaged in a struggle to the death, but, Teddy wanted to believe, the new frontier states were not stained by those ancient hatreds. They were, therefore, places in which the nation's psyche could repair itself. Obama, Brinkley believes, views his own polyglot story as a modern-day equivalent to that regenerative space identified by Roosevelt: as a way to heal or to transcend the black/white divide. And his writings and oratory act as a cerebral, virtual Wild West where that same healing mythology and space can be created.[8]

Obama grew up in post-statehood Hawaii knowing that he

was different, hearing repeatedly from his mother that his different-ness made him special. In *Kinship*, Wamba wrote of growing up in a white, middle-class community in Massachusetts in a home in which he was inculcated with pride in who he was. He was, he remembered, the only black kid in his class, was good natured, could read above grade level, and consequently was considered to be "a prized mascot who was encouraged to excel."[9] He could equally well have been writing about Barack Obama's youth.

After spending his teenage years as one of the few black students at Punahou, Obama then spent his young adulthood searching for his roots and working to create a coherent, compelling narrative that would explain his ancestry and build for himself a durable, tangible family from fragments. In large measure, that was the role played by community organizing and the Reverend Jeremiah Wright's Trinity United Church of Christ. Before he and Michelle had children and created their own family, Barack's fellow organizers and church members provided strong groups of people he could rely on in a way he couldn't with his own immediate family growing up. Institutions like the Gamaliel Foundation and the Industrial Areas Foundation are, says Harry Boyte, "a medium, a culture."[10] And like all cultures, they bond the individuals who make them up into a larger, more meaningful whole.

At Jeremiah Wright's church, Obama imbibed a version of Christianity that taught congregants to be proud of their racial and ethnic heritages, to be themselves rather than try to fit into personas molded by other cultures and individuals over the centuries. Before Wright became a liability for Obama, with politically incendiary sermons played endlessly on the nightly news during the spring of 2008, he was a messenger of hope for the young man. In Wright's version of Christianity, redemption wasn't something to be hoped for in the afterlife but was a living reality, a political aspiration to be worked toward here on earth. For a man with Obama's complex background and need for a grounded sense of identity, for a man who had spent his early adulthood in a continual quest for community, it was a compelling message. It was, in a way, a logical extension of the community organizing message he had himself been spreading since leaving Columbia University years earlier.

Later, his wife's family—stable, middle-class, structured in a way that his own family had never been—and then his and Michelle's two daughters, came to occupy the central role that community organizing had previously filled. He was determined that he would be a significant presence in his own children's lives in a way that his father had not been in his. "When I was a young man, I thought life was all about me—about how I'd make my way in the world, become successful, and get the things I want," Obama wrote in an open letter to Malia and Sasha, published in *Parade* magazine the week before his inauguration.[11] "But then the two of you came into my world with all your curiosity and mischief and those smiles that never fail to fill my heart and light up my day. And suddenly, all my big plans for myself didn't seem so important anymore. I soon found that the greatest joy in my life was the joy I saw in yours."

As a U.S. senator, Obama would return to Chicago to cook

barbecues in the backyard of the family's Hyde Park home on his daughters' birthdays. When his schedule permitted, he would take them to piano and tennis lessons and to school sports events. Living in a small apartment in Washington part of each week, he would discuss with reporters his sadness at being away from his children so much. And as a candidate for the presidency, that same anxiety—that sense of blues at not being home evenings to tuck the kids in—would periodically rear its head. In *The Audacity of Hope*, he had written about how, during the early years, with young children at home and a wife who felt sidelined, his political ambitions placed strains on his marriage. But then, at least, he was living in the same state as his family. A few years later, ensconced in D.C., if there was one drawback to the life of superstardom that was now his, it was the burden it placed on his role as a father.

Michelle Obama worried aloud about the impact that his candidacy for the presidency would have on their family. She told interviewers she feared it would be personally disruptive. She worried about how her children would handle all the attention. But then, she told *Glamour* magazine, she envisioned his being elected and ended up with "goose bumps."[12]

Barack Obama is, both by personality and as a strategic political choice, a conciliator, a community builder. Friends call him a pragmatic idealist, a radical moderate, or, sometimes, a moderate radical. He has ideals, but he has learned throughout his life that he needs to bring other people along with him if he is to achieve change. He has absorbed the lesson that success rarely comes to those too stubborn or rigid to acknowledge that many problems have more than one legitimate solution. That is why, when he was working to reform Illinois's death penalty process, in the wake of a series of police torture scandals and a slew of overturned death penalty convictions, he formed an alliance with Edward Petka, a conservative legislator who, as state's attorney in Will County, had earned the nickname Electric Ed by putting more people on death row than anyone else in Illinois history. "Barack would ask tremendous questions, pushing people to the limit, in a Socratic way," remembers Republican state senator Kirk Dillard, who attended the early morning Monday meetings Obama convened while working on the legislation. "He's very good at asking tough questions, and peppering people. But not making people mad who have different points of view, when he's finished asking, or barraging them with, these questions. It's a very good trait. He's witty. He has a pleasant and affable nature. But the type of questions that he asks, the way he probes is anything but affable. He has a gift for not alienating people who might be on the other side of the issue."[13] Being tough yet conciliatory is also how he was able to bring together liberals and conservatives in Springfield to successfully usher in the first ethics reforms in Illinois politics in a quarter century.

Yet despite his myriad friends and his strong, picture-postcard family, and despite his powerful ability to bring opposing factions and individuals together, on some level Obama is a loner. The president's background renders him instantly dissimilar to almost

all those who surround him. That doesn't make him lonely—
he is gregarious and charming, and has a finely honed, slightly
self-mocking sense of humor. But it does make him unlikely
to blend in with the crowd. As a young man, he wrote, he was
hounded by "the constant, crippling fear that I didn't belong
somehow, and that unless I dodged and hid and pretended to be
something I wasn't I would forever remain an outsider, with the
rest of the world, black and white, always standing in judgment."[14]

Perhaps because his heritage conspired to make him different, unique, much of Obama's own story is that of his search for
community. He writes about this at length in *The Audacity of Hope*,
describing an ongoing quest for a common set of values around
which to craft a more inclusive politics. "I think Democrats are
wrong to run away from a debate about values," the freshman
senator wrote. "As wrong as those conservatives who see values only as a wedge to pry loose working class voters from the
Democratic base. It is the language of values that people use to
map their world."[15] And yet he never seems fully absorbed into
any single community. There's a restless quality to his writings, a
sense that one part of him, at least, is always standing ready, bags
packed, waiting for a sign that it is time to move on. One of his
flaws, he writes, is "a chronic restlessness; an inability to appreciate, no matter how well things were going, those blessings that
were right there in front of me."[16]

At one point, he goes so far as to describe an earth-shaking,
existential moment at which he realized that he was "utterly
alone" in life.[17] His Kenyan half sister, Auma, told a reporter from

the British newspaper the *Guardian* that after meeting Barack for the first time, as a young adult, she realized "he can be in a room full of people and he withdraws on his own."[18] On another level, though, it renders him uniquely self-sufficient—"reflexive," according to Jerry Kellman—able to go solo when need be, to tough out the rough times, and to provide himself with counsel when—as in the Reverend Wright episode during the primary campaign, when he was called upon to disassociate himself from his longtime pastor—there are no ready scripts to adhere to.

Near the start of the financial implosion that would dominate the last months of the presidential election campaign, President Bush convened an emergency meeting attended by both Obama and Republican candidate John McCain, as well as a bevy of financial experts and other political leaders. In photos taken of that meeting, Obama sits three seats to the left of President Bush, a measurable distance separating him from the other key participants. His hands are clasped, and there's a look on his face not of disengagement but rather of emotional distance. These photos are dramatically different from the photos taken a couple months later at a White House meeting of all four living presidents—Jimmy Carter, George Bush Sr., Bill Clinton, and George Bush Jr.—in which Carter stands isolated and off to the side. Carter's isolation appears redolent of failure; at least in part he's alone because the others haven't made an effort to close the gap. Obama's aloofness, by contrast, both in this photograph and more generally, comes off as being the distance of the sage, a separateness that he has chosen rather than one foisted on him; and a distance that, paradoxically, at the end of the day allows him to be a unifier.

For Kellman, Obama's one-time mentor in the world of community organizing, that quality was crucial. For as long as he could remember, Obama had excelled in bringing opposing sides together. "The most important thing about Barack is how he deals with diversity, how he deals with pluralism. I saw that from the very beginning. Not only was he diverse in his own makeup, and had a very diverse set of experiences for a young man when I met him and interviewed him and got to know him, but he was good at dealing with diverse ideas and holding them together. Even opposing ideas—reconciling them. Pluralism, diversity, both biologically and in ideas, was the air that Barack breathes. It's his great gift. Part of that is, he had to deal with people's reactions to him his whole life. Both blacks and whites have reacted to Barack in a way that has to do with something other than who he is. His race has always been there. He's had to navigate diversity, and he's become gifted at that." In observing Obama over the years, Kellman had found him to be remarkably consistent in his methods. "He takes people who have stopped believing that more is possible and instills in them the belief that something more *is* possible; he takes people who disagree with one another, sometimes don't even like each other, and gets them to work together."[19]

Standing in front of the Democratic Party faithful at the Denver convention in which her husband was formally nominated to be the party's presidential candidate, Michelle Obama explained why she was confident that he would be an effective president.

"Barack doesn't care where you're from, or what your background is, or what party—if any—you belong to. That's not how he sees the world. He knows that thread that connects us—our belief in America's promise, our commitment to our children's future—is strong enough to hold us together as one nation even when we disagree."

In managing to tie the strands of his life together, in making whole a series of shards, Obama succeeded in carving a unique identity. The challenge that he extends to audiences follows from this: *If I can do this, if I can fuse Kenya and Kansas, Hawaii and Chicago, then surely you can too.*

CHAPTER THREE

SENSE OF HISTORY

Towering in the background, overlooking Obama's career as he has risen up the ladders of power, and illuminating his sense of political possibility, is the ghost of Abraham Lincoln, the "tall, gangly, self-made Springfield lawyer" conjured up as talisman during Obama's February 10, 2007, Springfield speech declaring his candidacy for the presidency of the United States. Or to be more accurate, the many ghosts of Lincoln: There is the great debater, the man made famous by his hours-long debates against Senator Douglas in 1858. There is the reluctant pragmatist, the leader who loathed slavery but gave over much of his first inaugural address to assuring Southerners of his willingness to countenance its continuation in the interests of saving the Union. There is the oratorical master, the visionary author of the Gettysburg Address. And then there is the idealist, the weaver of dreams of the Second Inaugural.

But Lincoln's ghosts never, for long, remain alone in their

sentry duty. When Obama speaks, the shades of Frederick Douglass, Franklin Delano Roosevelt, the Kennedy brothers, Martin Luther King, even Ronald Reagan rustle in the air around him. So, too, do an array of other historical figures, both American and foreign.

From an early age, Obama loved studying history, and later in life, he got immense pleasure from being considered a historical figure himself. During the midterm elections in 2006, a colleague of his and Michelle's neighbor, Jacky Grimshaw, who worked at the Center for Neighborhood Technology, made a countdown-to-the-election advent calendar. Behind each window, instead of a chocolate, was a quote from a famous historical personage. Behind window seventeen were some of Obama's words. Grimshaw showed him the calendar and, she remembered, his face simply lit up. He was as happy as a clam to be in the select historical club.

In November 2008, less than two weeks after the presidential election, *New Yorker* editor David Remnick wrote that Obama and other successful African Americans of his age group embodied a Joshua Generation.[1] They were, he posited, able to ride to power in a world shaped, and reshaped, by layers of sacrifice in decades and centuries past. That generation has high expectations—and why not? They believed, after all, that glass ceilings had been shattered, allowing them to reach for the sky. But it also has a tremendous sense of debt, of obligation to those who have come before. It is a generation imbued with both historical knowledge and a sense of historical mission.

In the mid-nineteenth century, the great African American orator and antislavery campaigner Frederick Douglass had urged America to look more carefully in the mirror, to see what he called the "fraud, deception, impiety and hypocrisy" of a people wedded to the liberty-proclaiming tenets of the Constitution yet at the same time tolerant of the continued existence of slavery.[2] He urged his fellow countrymen to make real the promises contained within America's founding documents. Only then, he told his audiences, would African Americans have a stake in the country, be able to celebrate Independence Day as their holiday too. For the Joshua Generation, that ability to celebrate the country as being theirs as much as anyone else's was finally being realized.

As a younger man, in an era transformed by the civil rights movement, Obama read and reputedly was much influenced by Mahatma Gandhi's autobiography; Gandhi had used moral suasion to undermine the Raj and drive the British out of India, to convince his fellow Indians that they had the ability to overturn colonial rule and successfully govern themselves. He had positioned himself as a healer and a unifier, a man able to transcend religious, tribal, and caste divides in pursuit of the dream of a free India. Obama also read the radical antifascist theologian Reinhold Niebuhr, author of the famous prayer, "God, give us grace to accept with serenity the things that cannot be changed, courage to change the things which should be changed, and the wisdom to distinguish the one from the other." He was active in student campaigns at Occidental College and Columbia University against the apartheid government of South Africa—presumably familiarizing himself with the words and writings of Nelson Mandela in the process.

In *Dreams from My Father*, Obama details his postadolescent fascination with the ideas of Malcolm X at a time in his life when he was flirting with black nationalism and deliberately shaping his persona to be somewhat akin to the self-proclaimed revolutionaries of the 1960s student movements a half generation earlier.

Later, in Chicago, his community organizing trainers immersed him in a people's history too often left forgotten. As examples they looked at what radical organizers had done in Appalachian Tennessee during the bleakest days of the Great Depression, when they developed a residential training center, for black and white alike, known as the Highlander School. Its founder, Myles Horton, intended it as a place in which young men and women would learn how to organize for better working conditions, affordable housing, and so on. They studied the life story of African American civil rights pioneer Ella Baker, who established scores of "citizenship schools" in postwar America, first on the islands dotting the South Carolina coast, then throughout the South. In these schools, young men and women would learn not just the importance of voting, but more generally the transformative power they could exert through broad civic participation, through letting their voices be heard. And they looked at the brave work of Bob Moses and other young Student Nonviolent Coordinating Committee organizers, who headed into the most violent counties of rural Mississippi in the early 1960s to live in poor African American communities and register to vote first one or two, then tens, then hundreds, and eventually hundreds of thousands of people.

"Whenever you want to really do something with somebody else then the first thing you have to do is make this personal connection, you have to find out who it is you're really working with," Moses told the University of Chicago scholar Charles Payne, when Payne was researching his book *I've Got the Light of Freedom.*[3] Change had to come, Moses and the other organizers believed, from the local level up.

Jacky Grimshaw thinks that her famous neighbor was likely also influenced by the deeds and thinking of Pope John XXIII, the man who ushered in Vatican II in the 1960s. The pope was a transformative figure, a leader who made the Catholic Church a far more inclusive, democratic institution—that, to take one example, allowed mass to be read in lay languages rather than solely in Latin—than it had been previously.

While Obama is fascinated by transformative leaders—he is, says one of his close friends, partial to the Great Man theory of history, to the idea that strong, charismatic individuals can chart the direction countries and civilizations take—it is the *interplay* of ideas and action that particularly intrigues him. Read Obama's writings and you are clearly reading the words of a man who loves grappling with social theories, but who also realizes the fragility both of ideas and of the social systems that rest upon them. Like most keen students of history, he understands the need for leaders to exhibit flexibility to meet changed circumstances. In his 2006 book, *The Audacity of Hope,* Obama wrote that "it may be the vision of the Founders that inspires us, but it was their realism, their practicality and flexibility and curiosity, that ensured the Union's survival."[4] Great men make history, but they are also made by it. They dream, but they also know how to get down to brass tacks.

America, for Obama, is a wondrous experiment, something to be marveled at rather than taken for granted. "At the core of the American experience are a set of ideals that continue to stir our collective conscience; a common set of values that bind us together despite our differences; a running thread of hope that makes our improbable experiment in democracy work," he wrote in *The Audacity of Hope.*[5] And yet at the same time, he is all too aware of the times in which the country—both leaders and populace—has strayed from its ideals. "Self-reliance and independence can transform into selfishness and license, ambition into greed and a frantic desire to succeed at any cost. More than once in our history, we've seen patriotism slide into jingoism, xenophobia, the stifling of dissent; we've seen faith calcify into self-righteousness, closed-mindedness, and cruelty toward others."[6]

Few politicians would dare to put such a critical analysis in print for public consumption. Yet always the criticism is tempered by a sense of possibility. Writing to his daughters in the open letter published in *Parade* magazine, Obama said of his grandmother Toot, "She helped me understand that America is great not because it is perfect but because it can always be made better—and that the unfinished work of perfecting our union falls to each of us."[7]

In his memoirs you sense a man who understands the human story as a continual series of journeys, of adventures; a saga of individuals and cultures searching for meaning, seeking to stamp their mark on the world as a way to escape their own fears of inconsequence. At moments, there's something almost quixotic about his understanding of the human condition. "Maybe once you stripped away the rationalizations, it always came down to a simple matter of escape," he wrote.[8] "An escape from poverty or boredom or crime or the shackles of your skin."

THE PAST IS NEVER REALLY PAST

In the caliber of his writing, in the ease with which he conjures up historical references, and in his ability to render the millennia-old human story as a living, breathing beast, Obama has often been compared to John F. Kennedy. "Kennedy liked to embellish his speeches with quotations from the widest possible variety of sources," wrote the thirty-fifth president's adviser and lead speechwriter, Ted Sorensen, in his book *Counselor*.[9] "Hemingway, Shaw, Aristotle, Socrates, Pericles, Demosthenes, Solon, and Pindar."

Nearly a half century later, Sorensen highly recommended his own lead researcher, Adam Frankel, to Barack Obama, and Obama hired the young man as his number two speechwriter, deputy to Jon Favreau, who had been speechwriting for first John Kerry and then Obama since graduating from the College of the Holy Cross in 2003. Periodically, as a doyenne in the world of presidential advisers, Sorensen would also offer confidential advice on turns of phrase to the young political superstar.

Sorensen has long claimed that he could write such powerful speeches for Kennedy because he thought like Kennedy; he knew what Kennedy wanted to say almost instinctually, almost before Kennedy himself knew. The same is true with Obama and Favreau, a president-speechwriter combo that will likely be analyzed for decades to come. The two talk together regularly, before Favreau writes major speeches, during the writing, and after the first draft has been submitted.

But the best speechwriters in the world couldn't make Obama deliver words with the poise and assuredness that he does. Witness the sorry delivery George W. Bush generally afforded to the words of his talented speechwriter, Michael Gerson. In part his oratory soars because, like John Kennedy and Winston Churchill, Obama often pens his own speeches—including his name-making speech to the Democratic National Convention in 2004 and his oration on race in America, delivered in Philadelphia nearly four years later. Like Churchill, who was known to call his secretaries in the small hours of the morning to take dictation for his speeches, Obama will work late into the night writing and rewriting until the words perfectly express the thoughts caroming around in his head.

Favreau knows the historical references Obama likes and has a confident understanding of what sources to plumb; he knows the tone his boss seeks to achieve in his oratory. And his boss, like Kennedy before him, has the intellectual apparatus and cultural references readily available to fine-tune an already good speech to make it mesh perfectly with the needs of the moment.

Obama, who belonged to a literary club at Punahou high school, for which he penned poems (reputedly of mediocre caliber) and short stories, told *Rolling Stone* magazine that he is a fan of Toni Morrison, the tragedies of William Shakespeare, and Ernest Hemingway.[10] In other publications, he has been quoted as saying he likes books by such writers as Aleksandr Solzhenitsyn, Herman Melville, Ralph Waldo Emerson, W.E.B. DuBois, Graham Greene, Doris Lessing, John Steinbeck, E. L. Doctorow, Philip Roth, and Studs Terkel.[11]

The great majority of Obama's favorite writers are realists, their writings grounded in experience, in the hard truths of life, rather than escapism and fantasy. Many of the themes these men and women write on—hardship, the overcoming of obstacles, corruption and intrigue, inequality, war, duty—are ones that Obama, in the political arena, has long been fascinated by. Read Solzhenitsyn or Steinbeck or, for that matter, Hemingway's epic Spanish Civil War novel *For Whom the Bell Tolls*, and you are brought face to face with great historical dramas, told through the stories of individuals. You are reading the narratives of everyday people writ large. For Obama, a community organizer who has spent a lifetime listening to people's stories and building a political career based partly on his own narrative talents, such writings are particularly evocative.

Like JFK, says Kennedy aide Richard Donohue, Obama is a man who can "create word pictures in your minds," using language to get audiences to visualize the events and dreams he is talking about.[12]

All of this stands in marked contrast to many contemporary politicians. John McCain, the Republican presidential candidate in 2008, might well have had a keen sense of military history, but his broader historical canvas was sadly shrunken. As for the party's vice presidential nominee, Alaska governor Sarah Palin, her sense of history seemed about as profound as her sense of foreign policy, which became the subject of late night TV jokes after she told interviewers that she had the capacity to deal with foreign leaders because residents of some Alaskan islands could see Russia from out their back doors.

What made Palin's ignorance more extraordinary was that the Republican Party attempted to define it as a plus, making her an all-too-average spokeswoman for "Joe Sixpack," in contrast to Obama's supposed elitism. Knowledge, according to this particular script, was for eggheads, not political leaders. Worse still, understanding the nuances of history was, somehow, un-American. It was, in many ways, the same vision of politics described a half century earlier by the political scientist Richard Hofstadter as the "paranoid style." In the nineteenth century, it had led to the self-proclaimed anti-immigrant Know-Nothing movement. In the 1950s, it had led to McCarthyism. This time around, however, it didn't work. Voters seemed eager for leadership that didn't talk down to them. Obama flourished, pushing a more cerebral, less sound-bite-based approach both to history and to politics, and peppering his speeches with historical references and imagery from America's past.

In Chicago's Grant Park, on the night of his election victory, Obama addressed a vast crowd of enthused supporters. The nation, he declared, needed to be remade; and the task would be carried out not just by a new administration but by a motivated populace, "the only way it's been done in America for 221 years— block by block, brick by brick, calloused hand by calloused hand."

Two days before Obama was sworn in, hundreds of thousands of people had gathered at the Lincoln Memorial to watch the pre-inauguration concert. On the giant screens flanking the east and west sides of the mall, images of ordinary Americans in workplaces around the country were projected. The great monuments making up the center of Washington, D.C., Vice President–elect Biden told the multitude, represented the "majesty of a great nation." And, he emphasized, that they were "all built stone by stone by American men and women."

On Inauguration Day, Obama took up the themes of sacrifice and duty. "Let us mark this day with remembrance," Obama told a worldwide audience on the day of his inauguration. "Of who we are and how far we have traveled. In the year of America's birth, in the coldest of months, a small band of patriots huddled by dying campfires on the shores of an icy river. The capital was abandoned. The enemy was advancing. The snow was stained with blood. At a moment when the outcome of our revolution was most in doubt, the father of our nation ordered these words be read to the people: 'Let it be told to the future world . . . that in the depth of winter, when nothing but hope and virtue could survive . . . that the city and the country, alarmed at one common danger, came forth to meet it.' America, in the face of our common dangers, in this winter of our hardship, let us remember these timeless words. With hope and virtue, let us brave once more the icy currents, and endure what storms may come."

And then he segued into an homage to American laborers. "For us," he declared, "they [past generations] toiled in sweatshops and settled the West; endured the lash of the whip and plowed the hard earth."

Shortly after Obama's speech, the forty-six-year-old Harlemborn poet and Yale professor Elizabeth Alexander rose to the podium to read "Praise Song for the Day," a poem she had been specially commissioned to compose based around a theme from Lincoln's Gettysburg Address: "that this nation, under God, shall have a new birth of freedom—and that government of the people, by the people, for the people, shall not perish from the earth."

It was a rare honor. Poets had only been asked to read their works at presidential inaugurations three times previously: in 1961, Robert Frost read at Kennedy's inauguration; and in 1993 and 1997, Bill Clinton's inaugurations featured readings by Maya Angelou and Miller Williams.

"Praise song for struggle, praise song for the day. / Praise song for every hand-lettered sign, / the figuring-it-out at kitchen tables," Alexander intoned. "We encounter each other in words, words / spiny or smooth, whispered or declaimed."

The Yale poet's lines, delineating the importance of everyday matters, of the small chores and joys, the loves and sorrows that make up daily routine, fit well the theme of the inauguration: that this was a new America, an administration that would listen to the voices of ordinary men, women, and children.

It was a carefully choreographed reminder to the global audience that historically America has been a country made great by underdogs. Its story can only be told and understood by digging beneath the surface, by searching for the lost stories of countless millions of "ordinary" people. If the Bush years had been characterized by a certain historical amnesia, the Obama years were, the inauguration's timbre made clear, to be framed by a powerful and inclusive sense of history.

For longtime activist and historian Harry Boyte, there was nothing accidental about all the majesty-of-labor imagery. It was, he believed, "a particular understanding of the American narrative. It is an interpretation of the American narrative that American society was built by ordinary people, by the labors of ordinary people, mostly unheralded, in a myriad of settings and ways. So in building towns and building communities and schools and festivals and libraries and public things—the commonwealth— as people developed and built the commonwealth, they became in a sense the commonwealth of citizens. So it's a strong work theme." It was, said Boyte, carefully redolent of Franklin Roosevelt, stressing, at a time when many millions were out of work, that ordinary workers constituted "the genius of America."[13]

"How might an agenda promoting public work encourage citizen health workers, teachers, clergy, business owners, trade union organizers, civil servants, and many others who work *with* their fellow citizens, not 'on' them?" Boyte and Carmen Sirianni, research director for new citizenship at Brandeis University, asked in an internal policy paper for the Obama campaign in the summer of 2008, the text of which was approved by the candidate personally.[14] "Public work is sustained effort by a mix of ordinary people who develop skills to work across differences to create things of lasting civic value."

MAKE ME DO IT

Having a wealth of historical knowledge at one's fingertips has its benefits. It means ready access to a mental bank filled with the treasures of world history and the ideas of its greatest thinkers. But in Obama's case, it goes beyond that. He doesn't simply have a good memory for historical dates and trivia or just know the names of a few important historians backed up by quotes from a few good books, Doris Kearns Goodwin's *Team of Rivals*, say, or Taylor

Branch's *Parting the Waters*. Rather, he grapples with contemporary events by trying to situate them historically—understanding their roots, their similarities and differences to events in the past, and their likely impact on the future. "On this earth one place is not so different from another—the knowledge that one moment carries within it all that's gone on before," Obama writes toward the end of *Dreams from My Father*.[15]

During the election campaign, he was asked by a supporter whether he could carve a peace in the Middle East. "Make me do it," he reputedly answered, echoing Franklin Roosevelt's advice to A. Phillip Randolph, one of the great trade union leaders of the prewar era, when Randolph pushed him to better protect the rights of America's workers.[16] Obama has the ambition to change the world; but he knows, from everything he has studied of the past, that a president succeeds in bringing about transformations when his supporters keep up their pressure for change rather than sitting back quiescently and waiting for him to do it alone.

America, he told a crowd of graduating seniors at Knox College, in Galesburg, Illinois, in June 2005, emerged as a "place where destiny was not a destination, but a journey to be shared and shaped and remade by people who had the gall, the temerity to believe that, against all odds, they could form 'a more perfect union' on this new frontier."[17] Within this framework, he clearly sees himself as a man of destiny, as someone with the ability to profoundly alter history, to shape that shared journey, rather than simply be swept along by it. "America," he told the students, "is a land of big dreamers and big hopes. It is this hope that has sustained us through revolution and civil war, depression and world war, a struggle for civil and social rights and the brink of nuclear crisis. And it is because of our dreamers that we have emerged from each challenge more united, more prosperous, and more admired than ever before."

Obama has declared in many conversations that it's not enough to simply be president, you have to aim at being a "great president." And that presumably means stamping one's mark on history. Unlike Karl Rove, however, who believed history could be bent entirely to a country's or an individual's whim, Obama understands that the making of history is a continual balancing act, a complex game of give-and-take. "There's a saying, 'There comes a time when the moment seizes you,'" explains Reverend Robert C. Jones Jr., another of Obama's friends and informal policy advisers. " 'And at that point you have the right to seize it back.' "

It is this ability to read historical trends that gave Barack Obama what seemed to be perfect-pitch political timing in the years following his ill-fated decision to try to unseat sitting Congressman Bobby Rush in a Democratic Party primary in 2000. That election (discussed later in the book) was the only defeat Obama ever experienced at the hands of voters. In the years following, he honed his political antennae and came to read the electorate's moods flawlessly. Obama believed, first in the run-up to the 2004 election and then during the long months in which he pondered entering the presidential race, that he had the chance to break the politics-as-usual mold. "He'd always felt as we look at the way things are being done politically between the Democrats and the Republicans and the Independents, that there just has to be a better way. There doesn't have to be that polarization. Someone can step up and bring these people together and move forward," explained Jones. By 2004, Obama felt that that someone was him, that the stars were aligning for a fundamental political transformation, and that he had the potential to be something of a national and international healer. The extraordinary response to his keynote address to the Democratic National Convention that summer only shored up his already strong sense of destiny calling. "The best possibility would be him," Jones believed his friend had concluded. "And the best possibility would be now."[18]

As the Bush presidency imploded a couple years later, that sense intensified. Obama believed in what he called, borrowing phrasing from his hero Martin Luther King, "the fierce urgency of now." The country was confronted by so many problems of such breadth and depth, he had concluded, that the normal paradigms no longer held. In such a moment, an African American man with a last name that rhymed with that of America's public enemy number one and a middle name the same as America's public enemy number two, could, however improbable the scenario might seem, be elected president of the United States.

HISTORY NEVER SITS STILL

Obama's interpretation of history is as a story in which progress prevails. It is, says Ted Sorensen, a saga of the gradual implementation of a state of "peace and justice,"[19] one in which humanity is continually moving, albeit in fits and starts, into a condition of greater liberty and potential better realized. If Richard Nixon was America's Machiavelli, Obama is more akin in his understanding of human aspirations to *The Rights of Man* author Tom Paine.

In that sense, Obama is a classic Enlightenment thinker. He believes in the notion of progress—the "precious journey towards that distant horizon," as he described it in his Knox College speech. And he believes in using the powers of rational governance, in alliance with an empowered citizenry, to push society along what Martin Luther King termed the "broad arc of justice."

"I know these are difficult times for America," Obama told a crowd in Canton, Ohio, in a speech one week before Election Day that was billed as his "closing argument" to voters. "But I also know that we have faced difficult times before. The American story has never been about things coming easy—it's been about rising to the moment when the moment was hard. It's about seeing the highest mountaintop from the deepest of valleys. It's about rejecting fear and division for unity of purpose. That's how we've overcome war and depression. That's how we've won great struggles for civil rights and women's rights and workers' rights. And that's how we'll emerge from this crisis stronger and more prosperous than we were before—as one nation; as one people."

For Heather Booth, a longtime organizer for social change and onetime director of the AFL-CIO's health-care-reform campaign, who first met Barack Obama during his voter-registration work

in Chicago in the early 1990s, the Illinois politi
represented an extraordinary historical moment.
she said, of a line from Seamus Heaney's poem
"once in a lifetime / the longed for tidal wave / of
up, / and hope and history rhyme."[20]

Obama thinks of power as a ball intercepted by different countries at different moments in time. No one holds it forever, and
no nation can remain militarily dominant during a period of
prolonged economic decline or growing economic inequality.
Like John Kennedy before him, who warned that the prosperity
of the few could not be secured when the many were left poor
and neglected, Obama declared in his inauguration speech that
"a nation cannot prosper long when it favors only the prosperous." Countries thrive, the president believes, when prosperity is
widely distributed; conversely, they decline when their protective
umbrellas fail to shield the vulnerable both within and outside
their borders.

Under George W. Bush, the United States had come to be
seen by many people around the world, and an increasing number of Americans too, as an ugly imperium; a country concerned
mainly with material wealth; a place of growing religious extrem-
ism, antiscientific dogmas, and military hubris. The United
States came to be seen too frequently as a country with its collective head in the sand, resentful of the opinions of others and
either unwilling or unable to navigate the complex cultural currents of the age. It was governed by people who, when the chips

ere down in the post-9/11 years, defended torture and adopted slash-and-burn policies on issues ranging from the environment to health care, from war to international relations. Worse still, it had leaders who adhered to the philosophy that America was no longer a mere player in the drama of history but instead its sole author. The great saga of human history had either concluded on America's terms—as in the famous post-1989 Francis Fukuyama thesis on the "end of history"—or was going to be permanently remolded in its image. "We're an empire now," a senior Bush aide, widely thought to be Karl Rove, said in the run-up to the invasion of Iraq. "And when we act, we create our own reality. And while you're studying that reality—judiciously, as you will—we'll act again, creating other new realities."[21]

Both theories involved a startling myopia, an assumption that the world would simply stand still while America froze its supremacy in place. Were the country not so powerful, it would have been a laughingstock; that it was so strong, so dominant on the world stage, made its hubris instead the focal point for growing international revulsion. Pew Research Center data detailed how solid majorities in previously pro-American countries like Germany came to have an unfavorable view of the United States under George Bush. In the Muslim world, America's approval ratings in some countries were in the single digits.

To Obama, the ways in which the Bush administration interacted with the rest of the world appeared fatally flawed. Obama's unique family background allowed him to claim roots and connections in America, Africa, Asia, and Europe; and in searching for his identity during his early adulthood, he had traveled the world and spent years coming to understand his, and America's, place within it. He had thought long and hard about how the United States should project its extraordinary power in the twenty-first century.

Obama was by no means an isolationist, but his foreign policy ideal was closer to that of his adviser, Harvard professor Samantha Powers—who believed in a foreign policy grounded in respect for human rights and the imperative of using American power to prevent genocide in regions such as Darfur—than it was to the neoconservative empire builders of the early years of the century. Instinctually he was closer to the mind-set of Franklin Roosevelt—who articulated a case for intervention against fascism by delineating the "four freedoms" that American armaments and military alliances ought to support, the "moral order" at the heart of the American story.[22] He was more comfortable with the idealistic side of American foreign policy represented by, say, John F. Kennedy's Peace Corps than with the swaggering politics of Bush and Cheney. Powers, author of *A Problem from Hell: America and the Age of Genocide*, told *Rolling Stone* magazine's Ben Wallace-Wells in early 2007, "He doesn't get weighted down by the limits of power, . . . But he sees you have to grasp those limits in order to transcend them."[23]

The mature Obama is still very much in tune with the young Obama, whose undergraduate thesis at Columbia was on nuclear disarmament. As a world leader, he would be willing to countenance an assertive U.S. military doctrine but only as part of a much broader strategy of alliance-building and the winning over of hearts and minds. "To those who cling to power through corruption and deceit and the silencing of dissent, know that you are on the wrong side of history," Obama declared in his inauguration speech, "but that we will extend a hand if you are willing to unclench your fist." Two weeks into his presidency, his administration announced that the United States and Russia would sit down together to negotiate far-reaching reductions in the two countries' nuclear weapons stockpiles.

America would remain strong, thought Obama, for so long as the world revered American ideals; for so long as large parts of the world *wanted* America as their guardian angel. It would ultimately fail if—like the now-defunct USSR—it surrounded itself with surly satellite states, and dependent peoples, who paid homage to America not out of any ideological sympathy but simply out of fear. In the preface that Obama composed for the 2004 edition of *Dreams from My Father,* he wrote of the dangers of a world in which wealth gaps were widening and the wealthy either ignored the despair of the poor or "when the disorder spills out of its proscribed confines, [applied] a steady, unthinking application of force, of longer prison sentences and more sophisticated military hardware . . . I know that the hardening of lines, the embrace of fundamentalism and tribe, dooms us all."[24] In *The Audacity of Hope*, Obama wrote, "At times, American foreign policy has been farsighted, simultaneously serving our national interests, our ideals, and the interests of other nations. At other times American policies have been misguided, based on false assumptions that ignore the legitimate aspirations of other peoples, undermine our own credibility, and make for a more dangerous world."[25]

The youth of President Obama's father, Barack Obama Sr., straddled the end years of British colonial rule in Kenya. His story was inextricably intertwined with one system's collapse and another's messy birth. He was a technocrat educated at elite Western universities to play a role in governing newly independent Kenya; yet he was also a Luo tribesman on the wrong side of ugly internal divides within that new governing system. He was a sharply intelligent man ultimately brought low because of his unwillingness to compromise with figures he believed to be stupid or corrupt or both. In searching for his father's legacy, Obama discovered the story of a man who spent long years in a form of domestic purgatory, barred from the top jobs his talents qualified him for, oftentimes reduced to conditions of humiliating poverty.

Having grown up steeped in his family legends—of his grandfather's first encounters with Europeans, of the upending of the village hierarchies and age-old certainties brought by colonialism, of the scramble for power that his father witnessed after the British Empire crumbled—Obama understands the rapidity with which seemingly solid governing structures can break apart; he viscerally knows the finite nature of empire, the tales of hope—and also of woe—that play out as countries rise and fall. Obama understands, as perhaps few modern presidents have, the fragility of social systems, and also of individuals caught in the web of history.

"As Britain knows, all predominant power seems for a time invincible, but, in fact, it is transient. The question is: what do you leave behind?" British Prime Minister Tony Blair asked his audience during an historic address to both Houses of Congress, in Washington, D.C., on July 17, 2003. It is a question that Obama—now at the pinnacle of power in a country that occupies a role on the global stage comparable to that played by Britain in the last decades of its dominance—has been trying to answer his whole political career. *How do you wield power wisely? How do you use the fleeting windows of opportunity opened by that power to create a better country and a better world?*

Of course, to even ask those questions of himself, Obama had to have considerable confidence in his own abilities to gain that power in the first place, to harness America's energies in pursuit of his own visions of progress.

CHAPTER FOUR

SELF-CONFIDENCE

In 1997, not long after arriving in Springfield as a state senator, Barack Obama was approached by a much older colleague, a feisty Irish American named Denny Jacobs. Jacobs enjoyed the shock value he could impart to his words, and he delighted in telling the freshman that he didn't belong in Springfield. Obama looked shocked, even angry. *Was it a racial snub? Was this man picking a fight with him?* No, no, Jacobs reassured him, impishly pleased at the impact his words had had; he only meant that he'd been watching Obama, listening to him at committee meetings, and Obama was too smart for the state capital. The politicians in Springfield wouldn't appreciate his talents. He was, said Denny, destined for bigger things. The answer seemed to satisfy Obama, and he and the older man, a hard-drinking, fast-talking, wheeler-dealing downstate politician from the little town of East Moline, on the Mississippi River—and a man who gloried in speaking out in defense of the culture of backroom deals—somewhat improbably became fast friends.

Soon afterward, Obama was admitted to a select group of poker-playing senators, an all-male, bipartisan club that met for evenings of card games at the house of state senator Terry Link. *How did he get admitted to the game?* Well, says Denny, "Barack has that easy little laugh, that easy little smile. Let's call it his winning smile. He's an easygoing guy who isn't afraid to say, 'Hey, I understand you play a little poker. Let's get together and play a little poker.' He gives you that little smile and says, 'Yeah, I'm on.' And they say, 'Yeah, you're on,' and include him in. The guy, he's just a guy; and coming from my vernacular and my area, where I was born and raised, to me that's number one. If you're just a good old guy or a good old gal, that's what you are. And that's what President Barack is, he's just a good guy."

And so the young, African American, anti-machine politician from liberal Hyde Park began playing a regular poker game with a group of older, more conservative white men from rural Western and Southern Illinois. They might argue about abortion or gun control in between hands, but these men would ultimately become some of Obama's biggest fans, and some of his earliest, and most crucial, endorsers when he decided to run for the U.S. Senate in 2003.[1]

The senators would bet quarters up to a few dollars and play everything from Texas Hold 'Em to Pass the Trash and Baseball. On a big night, someone might walk away with a few hundred dollars. The game would start around seven thirty. Obama would generally show up a couple of hours late, after first going out to eat. And he would stay till well after midnight, slowly smoking his way through four or five Marlboros during the course of the evening. Occasionally he'd have a beer, more often a diet soda. He preferred traditional poker, either a five- or seven-card straight game, and he took great pleasure in winning. "He was very, very conservative in his approach," Jacobs found. "Whenever push came to shove, you never really knew what he had. He was a good bluffer. He didn't bluff very often. He didn't bluff a lot, so whenever he *did* bluff, he'd do pretty well, because people didn't consider him a bluffer." Conversely, when others tried to bluff him, he was a hard man to con. "He wouldn't take a bluff. He would stay in, and you had to show him. You see so many people, if you throw a bluff at them, they throw up their hands and say, 'Oh my God!' But Barack, he's going to see it through."

RENDEZVOUSING WITH DESTINY

One of Obama's close friends remembers Barack and Michelle coming in to a party at the White House on the evening of his inauguration. The jazz musician Wynton Marsalis was playing. Obama, said his friend, entered the magnificent room with not an iota of self-doubt, with no nerves, no sense of awe at his grandiose new living quarters. "Obama seemed like he was born for it, like 'I'm meant to be here.'" He could, the friend felt, walk the hallways of power with utter ease.

Perhaps it was that bubble of effortlessness that Michelle was gently trying to deflate during the early days of the primary campaign when she told readers of *Glamour* magazine that her husband was "snore-y and stinky" in the mornings. "Barack is very much human," she told the interviewer. "So let's not deify him." And yet she also believed passionately that "he has something special to offer the political process."[2]

"He leaves no doubt that he thinks highly of his own abilities—and rightly should. It's not that he says, 'You know, I'm a hotshot,'" explained one of Obama's erstwhile colleagues, attorney George Galland. "That's just not how he is. And he doesn't tend to start talking about all the things he knows so that he can impress you with how much he knows. So it isn't what he says. But I don't think anyone who ever dealt with Barack ever had any doubt he was plenty confident that he was an unusually talented person and would go plenty far. We all know people like that. And usually they're right."[3] It was manifested, thought Galland, in a host of little signals; he wouldn't talk himself down, his speech patterns didn't exhibit personal insecurities. "I never saw an insecure bone in his body, to tell you the truth."

Geoff Stone, a University of Chicago law professor who was serving as dean when he first met the young Obama, recalled that he was left with an impression of "someone who was very much at ease with himself. Body language is an apt part of it, tone of voice, a sense of—I don't want to say command; that would be slightly inaccurate. But a sense of being an equal when he's meeting with the dean of a law school when he's still a law student."[4] Over the years, Stone observed a man with a great "openness to ideas, the willingness to test propositions rather than to assert them as definitive," and the knowledge that history is littered with casualties of good intentions, people and movements who meant well but didn't think through their ideas carefully enough, who were felled by the law of unintended consequences.

Perhaps because of his strong sense of history as well as his unorthodox family background, Obama radiates confidence not just in his own abilities but in the ability of the country to adapt to his presence and to his ideas. When supporters held a fundraiser for Obama in Cambridge, Massachusetts, in the fall of 2003, Harvard law professor David Wilkins, one of the few African Americans on the law-school faculty, took him aside and asked, "Barack, you don't *really* think you can win do you?" Wilkins was from Chicago; his mother lived in Obama's state senate district. It was, felt Wilkins, pie in the sky to believe that a black man could win a U.S. Senate race in Illinois. "Yes, I do," Obama answered, and proceeded to explain a detailed strategy of coalition building that he had calculated would propel him to victory.[5] When advisers urged him to sit the 2008 presidential election out, saying that he was too young and inexperienced and that the country wasn't "ready" for a black president, Obama responded by politely but firmly disagreeing, declaring that 2008 was his moment, that a unique confluence of events was paving the way for his victory.

Obama believes in the need to reinvigorate American democracy—and by that he understands far more than simply encouraging higher voter turnout. Elections alone aren't sufficient to instill democracy in a country, the president-elect told a *Washington Post* editorial board meeting a few days before his inauguration, in a conversation on foreign policy. His answer, however, said as much about his domestic philosophy as his ideas regarding international engagement. Elections, he argued "are one facet of a liberal order, as we understand it. So in a lot of countries the first question is—if we go back to Roosevelt's four freedoms—the first question is freedom from want and freedom from fear. If people aren't secure, if people are starving, then elections may or may not address those issues. But they're not a perfect overlap."[6] Rather, for Obama, elections are one part of a larger continuum that involves ongoing mass civic participation; his vision of democracy revolves around promoting a communal ethos, a sense of responsibility for the common weal. "The values prized [by the Founding Fathers]," wrote community organizing guru Harry Boyte in *Free Spaces*, "included service to the community, frugality, hard work, independence, and self-restraint. Their opposites—extravagance, self-indulgence, idleness, and so forth—had no place in a virtuous and just republic."[7] In energizing tens of millions of Americans, young people in particular, with a Kennedy-esque call to service, and in dramatically expanding service programs such as Americorps, Obama believes he can raise once more the pillars of that just republic.

HARD KNOCKS AND LUCKY BREAKS

The grand ambitions work well on the national and international stage, on a dais in Berlin, say, addressing hundreds of thousands of adoring supporters, or onstage at a sports stadium in Denver, a forest of cell-phone cameras pointed upward at him from the audience below. In smaller, less august venues, the self-confidence Obama has always exhibited can come off differently—as arrogant, even pretentious. Obama's biographer, David Mendell, writes of a man who can be "imperious, mercurial, self-righteous and sometimes prickly."[8] At times when he is describing Obama's early post-Harvard political career, he almost makes his subject sound as if he is touched with an at least mild case of megalomania. "He is an extraordinarily ambitious, competitive man with persuasive charm and a career reach that seems to have no bounds," opined the biographer. "He is, in fact, a man of raw ambition so powerful that even he is still coming to terms with its full force."[9] *Newsweek* reporter Evan Thomas, in his book *A Long Time Coming,* recounts a small meeting in South Carolina when then-Senator Obama started boasting, telling his audience he didn't need to prove himself, that he had already made it, that he had already been on Oprah's show. The candidate, wrote Thomas, came off as cocky, and he almost lost his audience.

It was a trait Obama had worked hard to overcome since winning election to the Illinois Senate over a decade earlier. While the poker-playing crowd loved him, others were less sanguine. The young state senator, remembered John Cameron, a longtime staffer for Citizen Action and currently political director for the Illinois branch of the AFSCME trade union, came off as "pretentious," as a man who was "insufferably ambitious," desperate to speed away from the somewhat limited world of Springfield politics. The first time Cameron met Obama, his tiny ground-floor office at the State capitol building—freshman senators from the minority party always received almost unusably small workspaces—was filled with boxes of copies of *Dreams from My Father*, recently sent from New York by his publishers. *Publishing your own autobiography at age thirty-four, you think that's not in-your-face arrogance?* Cameron recalls thinking angrily. *Who is this guy? He's just a kid and he's already written his autobiography.*

In the rough-and-tumble world of Illinois machine politics, Obama appeared to be holier-than-thou, a Mother Teresa type who didn't like to schmooze with too many colleagues, who wrapped all his decisions up in a language of ethical purity, and who couldn't wait to jump in his car and return home to Michelle. "I have to honestly say that in that period I thought he was more pretentious than real. I was less than an enthusiastic admirer," said Cameron. "This is a guy, he'd sit in committee and roll his eyes if he thought the testimony was below him. He'd be impatient to move things through the legislative process. His demeanor and the way he came across at that point seemed very off-putting."[10]

Many African American state senators, longtime local big shots like Rickey Hendon and Donne Trotter, felt the new kid on the block was too big for his boots, too cocksure, too eager for the spotlight. Trotter was much quoted as saying that Obama was a white man in a black face; Hendon, who felt Obama hadn't paid his dues by coming up in an impoverished inner city, got into a couple of well-publicized shouting matches with the newcomer. Onlookers remember, with some glee, that the pair almost came to blows once. In general, thought his critics, he seemed too aloof, unwilling to blend in with the crowd.

The whole persona was, according to Cameron, "immature." It was full of a "certain male style of brashness," the kind of brashness that worked when he was genially trash-talking fellow attorneys on the golf course but didn't necessarily go over well in the halls of power in a place like Springfield, Illinois. Obama, the Citizen Action staffer felt, was a man heading for a fall.

Luckily for Obama, a man itching to make it to D.C., the fall came early and didn't do him any long-term damage. Obama decided to challenge a sitting U.S. Congressman, Bobby Rush, in the Democratic primaries in 2000, and he ended up being hammered. Rush, a onetime Black Panther, essentially accused Obama of treading on his turf, of being an Ivy League–educated Hawaiian carpetbagger with no real feeling for the life of inner-city African Americans. Fair or not, the charges stuck. Without a coalition of local supporters behind him, Obama couldn't effectively retaliate. Worse still, then-president Bill Clinton campaigned hard on Rush's behalf, going so far as to record a radio spot urging voters to stick with him. Come primary day, Obama didn't just lose by a whisker; he was trounced, losing to the incumbent by over thirty percent. (While Obama isn't known to hold grudges, his neighbor, Jacky Grimshaw, thinks it at least possible that his clear distaste for Bill Clinton dates back to this election and to Obama's feeling that Clinton handed him his head on a platter.)[11]

These days, Rush, the only politician to ever beat Obama electorally, won't talk about the primary. He has, his office says, put the past behind him and is now a friend of the president's. Back in 2000, however, he wasn't reluctant to talk. "He went to Harvard and became an educated fool," the journalist Ted Kleine quoted Rush as saying, in an article in the *Chicago Reader* in March 2000. "We're not impressed with these folks with these eastern elite degrees."[12] He also accused the young state senator of being something of an armchair warrior, a man who talked the talk about equality but had never been willing to demonstrate and protest and kick up a fuss to rile the establishment.

The defeat was one of the low points of Obama's public life. But it was also a eureka moment. When the numbers were analyzed, the contours of the loss suggested two things: One, Obama was not a natural "black politician." In a race for black votes in a majority black district, he was vulnerable to the "outsider" charge. Two, among the white voters in the congressional district, Obama had emerged a favorite. He had, apparently, terrific crossover appeal, especially for female white voters.

A few years later, when David Axelrod's consulting firm, AKPD Media, ran a series of focus groups with white, middle-class voters, the response to video footage of Obama talking about his life story was extraordinary. "'Be still, my beating heart,'" Axelrod's partner, John Kupper, remembers one woman saying. "He connected at a visceral level with these folks," explained Kupper. The firm, whose clients had included Harold Washington, had never before had a candidate with such crossover appeal.[13]

Many observers of Obama's political career have concluded that the loss in the Congressional race ultimately paved the way for the making of a viable presidential candidate. First, it taught him the importance of reaching out to a broad base. Second, while he lost the election, he won a significant number of white votes, a fact his handlers a few years later would realize held the key to his electoral viability. Third, the humiliating loss tempered his rougher edges. It was, thought Cameron, a godsend. "Frankly, it certainly made him a better politician, and a more pleasant person to be around, hopefully a better human being. He needed the humbling lesson: It's not about you; it's about you *and* the voters." In the years following, Cameron became a loyal fan of the rising politician. He had grown into his outsize talents and was, thought Cameron, now ready for the big-time.

To be a great politician, Cameron believed, one had to have empathy in addition to self-assurance. Friends from his community-organizer days believed that Obama had always had the former. There was the time, remembered Mike Kruglik,[14] one of his Gamaliel Foundation mentors, when he sat down with a young lady from the Altgeld Gardens public housing projects, and talked with her for hours about what she wanted to do with her life. He listened to her story, realized she had skills and ambitions that could move her beyond the impoverished circumstances she was in, and convinced her she had the ability to get a college degree. That, said Kruglik, epitomized the community organizer's creed of working with local residents to achieve personal transformation.

But, did having a good ear compensate for what many of his new colleagues in the state capital saw as an overweening sense of self-importance? Outside the world of community organizing, in the late 1990s many Springfield political figures, especially Democrats wary of his abilities and the likelihood that he would leapfrog them in his race to the top, shared Cameron's suspicions. In the minds of his critics, Obama's self-confidence and his sense of destiny, if they weren't toned down, would be his undoing. With hindsight, they were, of course, wrong. Eight years after losing to Bobby Rush, Obama would be elected president of the United States.

CAMPAIGN PLANES, GROCERY STORES, AND HOT IRONS

In his memoirs, Obama admits to a powerful fear of losing. "Not just fear of losing—although that is bad enough—but fear of total, complete humiliation. I still burn, for example, with the thought of my one loss in politics, a drubbing in 2000 at the hands of incumbent Democratic Congressman Bobby Rush," then-Senator Obama wrote. "Most of the other sins of politics are derivative of this larger sin—the need to win, but also the need not to lose."[15] In a weak man, such a fear could all too easily result in paralysis. In a man of Obama's talents, however, it simply fueled his ambitions. Always somewhat restless, the bitter taste of that defeat propelled him to always look to the future, to seek higher ground from which it would be that much harder to be dislodged. Yes, he was already a state senator in his middle thirties, but he wanted to head to D.C. Yes, he was a U.S. Senator at the age of forty-three, but he felt, somehow, the ride wasn't yet over.

When good things happened, he'd take them in stride, seeming to assume they were no more than his due. This was made strikingly apparent to his neighbor, Jacky Grimshaw, in the spring of 2004. Obama was running for the U.S. Senate and had been introduced to Democratic presidential nominee-apparent John Kerry at a local fundraiser. Kerry was so impressed with the young man that he asked him to accompany him on his campaign plane on a whirlwind tour of Illinois. News reports from the trip portray Obama as at times outshining the Massachusetts senator. Be that as it may, it was in the wake of this successful collaboration that Kerry invited Obama to give his now-famous keynote speech at the party's national convention that summer in Boston.

Afterward, talking over their backyard fences while Obama smoked a cigarette on his porch, Grimshaw asked him what the experience was like. She was excited; after all, it wasn't every day that one's neighbor got invited onto a presidential campaign plane. "Barack was very laid-back," she recalled, with some wonder, nearly five years later.[16] "Not gushing. There was no tremendous sense of excitement or anything like that. He was, like, 'Yeah, we did a bunch of stuff.' It was so matter of fact, which is just typical of him." Grimshaw remembered that his tone of voice in describing the trip with Kerry was just about the same as his tone later in the conversation when he mentioned that Michelle had asked him to go down to the corner store to pick up some groceries. "They were kind of, like, equal events in his life. It's just him, it's just his personality." She stops and laughs at the bizarre recollection. Obama recognized the honor Kerry had accorded him, but he'd taken the whole episode completely in stride. He was, Grimshaw believed, congenitally even-keeled, a man completely "comfortable in his skin," and radiating "internal strength."

Periodically during these years, he'd phone his friend Reverend Alvin Love and ask for advice. *Should I run for this office? Am I on the right track here?* He'd always ask Love to pray for him, and would listen silently as his friend sought God's blessings for his endeavors. Obama, the pastor felt, had a "deeply personal" relationship with his God; he wasn't one to get involved in denominational battles, and he wasn't one to try to impose his beliefs on others, but hearing those prayers seemed to lighten his load. They helped him maintain his legendary calm.

In December 2006, Love was sitting around his house when he got another of those calls. Obama told him that he was thinking of throwing his hat in the ring to be the Democratic Party's presidential nominee. "My initial advice," Love recalled, in his deep, baritone voice, "was 'I don't know if I can give you any advice about running for president.'" Then the pastor thought about it some more and pulled up a recommendation his own father had given him decades earlier. "Son, you have to strike while the iron is hot." Obama reputedly replied, "Revved up, Love, the iron can't get much hotter." "I just laughed," said Love. A few weeks later, his friend called him again, this time to tell him he had decided to seek the nomination.[17]

During the primary season in 2007–8, even when the poll numbers suggested otherwise, Obama could sense momentum was building for his candidacy. "Do not get attached to the polls," he reputedly told his senior advisers.[18] "Polls give us a snapshot of the past. I want to go into the fourth quarter tied, jump ball, and I know we can take it."

That drive to success had long been a core part of who Obama was. Leon Despres, a one-hundred-year-old doyen of Chicago's progressive community—as a middle-aged lawyer with a history of having been a Socialist Party member during the Great Depression, Despres had won election as an alderman to the Fifth Ward, in 1955, on an anti-machine platform—believed he had an "extraordinary ambition."[19] And, he said, he didn't mean that in a pejorative way; Obama was, Despres felt, as driven as Franklin Roosevelt or John Kennedy, but he channeled more of his ambition into good causes and less into personal self-aggrandizement. Now, in 2007–8, No Drama Obama would finally see whether his cool, unruffled exterior would help propel him to the White House, to the pinnacle of power.

CHAPTER FIVE

POISE

Throughout the early years of his adulthood, Obama's poise, his sense of presence, amazed acquaintances. Many people recollect meeting him when he was still unknown and coming away so impressed that they told their spouses or colleagues that they had just met a man who could—no, make that *would*—one day be president. Some of that might be simple wishful thinking; people seeing a man they had once brushed shoulders with emerge as president and wanting so badly to believe they'd predicted greatness decades earlier that they generate rose-tinted memories to that effect. But too many people say this for it all to be hype.

"The main thing I remember from that day," said Jackie Kendall, an organizer with the renowned Midwest Academy, of her first meeting with Obama in the mid-1980s, "when I went home that night, I said to my husband 'I just met a kid who someday we're going to say *We knew him when.*' He was that good."[1]

John Milner, a longtime police chief from the Chicago suburb of Elmhurst, who went on to become a Republican state senator, met Obama while he (Milner) was cochair of Fight Crime: Invest in Kids–Illinois, a group that brought together law enforcement people and social reformers around the issue of juvenile crime. "I was trying to promote quality preschool education, quality after-school programs. We brought together police chiefs, sheriffs, prosecutors, and families of victims. We came together and began to advocate for these quality preschool and after-school programs." Not all of the legislators they met understood the linkages between these programs and crime reduction. But "when I met Barack, this guy got it immediately. I was impressed by his ability to demonstrate his openness, his willingness to listen, and his look of genuineness. He had good eye contact, he nodded his head. I felt as though this guy is connecting with me, very swiftly. It's a gift, it's an important gift."[2] So smitten was the conservative police chief with the young, liberal politician that he took his police deputy aside and told him he had just talked with a man who could one day live in the White House.

A television screenwriter from Los Angeles visiting Chicago to research community organizing groups was so impressed by seeing Obama in action that he postponed his return flight and spent a week shadowing Obama at neighborhood meetings. One evening, toward the end of his stay, he leaped onstage and told the bemused audience that, mark his words, their organizer would one day be the United States' president.[3]

When Stephen Heintz, currently president of the Rocke-feller Brothers Fund and chairman of the board of the progressive New York–based think tank Demos, flew to Chicago with his colleague Charlie Halpern to talk with Obama about his joining Demos's board in its early days, they met for breakfast at an elite social club. "He was not wearing a jacket and tie, was wearing a leather jacket, looking very cool," said Heintz. "Even at this first meeting, when he was still very young, he had this certain kind of cool intensity. There's this interesting counter-play. He's very cool, but he's also very intense. There's this real firm awareness and intensity and drive that comes through in this very cool manner. And that's an interesting combination. We were both taken with him and eager to have him on the founding board of Demos. We walked out of the meeting saying, 'My God, this is an incredible young man. This looks like the kind of guy who could one day be the first African American president of the United States.'" Independently, Halpern corroborated his friend's recollection.[4]

That so many people came away with this impression can't be explained simply by talking about Obama's intelligence or knowl-edge or professional demeanor. Lots of people exhibit these quali-ties, yet they aren't immediately labeled presidents in the rough. There was something else going on here; something almost intan-gible. In the same way as Marilyn Monroe, the quintessential It Girl, exuded a sexuality not reducible to the sum of her body parts, so Obama's leadership qualities couldn't be reduced to a mere list of personality traits.

——

At least some of this magnetism is a by-product of skills that the young Barack Obama brought with him into Harvard Law School and there honed to perfection. Harvard Law School is, after all, one of the American elite's premier training institutions, as much a proving ground for ambitious would-be politicians as a boot camp for aspiring corporate lawyers. The school plays a role in U.S. political leadership culture akin to Balliol College, Oxford, or King's College, Cambridge, in England, and to the Sorbonne or the Ecole Nationale d'Administration in Paris. And the *Harvard Law Review,* of which Obama was elected president in 1990, serves to cultivate standout leaders within this already small, self-contained world of overachievers.

The *Review* has a separate headquarters, a small white-painted building named Gannett House, away from the main law school, near the university gym. And it has its own century-old traditions and rituals. There is, for example, the election process itself, a day-long affair in which presidential hopefuls have to cook meals for all their colleagues as they engage in a series of ever-tenser elimination ballots. Then there's the annual *Revue,* a written parody distributed at an event at the Harvard Club in Boston, somewhat akin to the Washington, D.C., Gridiron Club dinner, at which the staff boisterously skewers the top editor. The year Obama was president, his colleagues enthusiastically mocked his multicultural persona, asserting that he was the Norwegian progeny of a part-time fisherman and a backup singer for Abba who had somehow "discovered" that he was black when exposed to life in urban Chicago. The *Revue* made Obama sound something like a film negative version of Steve Martin's *The Jerk*—a white man who grows up in a black family thinking he is black, only to belatedly discover that he isn't African American after all. Being able to roll with the intellectual punches, to wryly laugh at oneself and to emerge the stronger for it—these were traits Harvard's top law students inculcated as surely as they did a knowledge of the law.

Good lawyers, said David Wilkins, emerged from the law school with the ability to speak well. *Great* lawyers came out with the ability to also listen well, to hear what others were saying and to adapt accordingly.[5]

At the time Obama was sworn in as U.S. President, one in ten U.S. Senators were graduates of Harvard Law School, as were five of the nine Supreme Court Justices. If they shared a single trait that transcended their ideological differences, it was a sense almost of noblesse oblige toward the American Constitution; its words and its sentiments were theirs to understand, to protect, and to nurture.

Obama is "deeply read in the American legal tradition and the American constitutional tradition," says Douglas Baird, the University of Chicago law professor responsible for hiring the young Obama as a lecturer to teach classes on constitutional law after he returned to the Windy City from Harvard. He isn't familiar with just the Cliff Notes version of, say, the Emancipation Proclamation; instead, he's actually read, and internalized, the nitty-gritty small print. Similarly, he has studied Supreme Court decisions such as *Roe v. Wade* in great detail and informed himself not just on the political sound bites surrounding them but on their underlying constitutional implications. These were the stuff of water-cooler conversations for Obama and his colleagues at the University of Chicago.

STAYING CALM AMID STORMS

Combine innate self-confidence with an assuredness of one's personal destiny, add the leadership and analytical skills so carefully cultivated by institutions such as Harvard Law School and the University of Chicago, throw in good looks, stirring oratorical talents, and the ability to carefully listen to other people, and you have the makings of a powerhouse.

Once installed on the Demos board, Obama quickly made his mark. He was always "a very distinct individual in the room," Stephen Heintz observed. "Part of it is his aura, his charisma. Part of it is, I think there is a little bit of an aloofness. You don't see him as being really chummy with people in a meeting. He interacts in a very businesslike kind of way. A serious way. Not that he's cold or doesn't have a sense of humor. But there is a sense of a slight bit of aloofness. A kind of guarding his distinct place in the conversation. Unlike others, whom you experience in a more easygoing, collegial style. His is a little more individualistic in a group setting. He was very respectful, interested, a good listener, wanted to make his points forcefully and articulately when he was ready to, but he was very good at listening to others; he didn't feel he needed to dominate the conversation. He's certainly *not* a backslapper, old-style real warm kind of politician. A complete contrast to George Bush. He's not the kind of guy who will come up with a nickname for everyone in the room. His style is more formal, without being stiff."

Demos wasn't alone in wanting Obama on its board. His calmness, the sense he projected of being in control, was magnetic. In Chicago, the Joyce Foundation, the Woods Fund, and then the Annenberg Challenge all brought him on, despite the fact that he was only a young man barely out of his twenties with a mountain of law school debt still to pay off.

Even when it came to grieving, that most elemental of human emotions, Obama knew how to separate his private feelings from his public presence. When his mother was dying of cancer, he was devastated. Friends believe that in some ways her death is still an open wound to him, something too painful to fully confront. Yet he didn't take time off work, and he refused to let his performance slip. To his boss, Judson Miner, his controlled grief came off as "dignified." Always, he felt, when you were in Obama's presence, "you were very much aware of his stature." Even when he consulted George Galland on how to navigate the morass of health insurance bureaucracy to secure his mother the treatments she needed for her ovarian cancer during the last months of her life—circumstances tailor-made to smash even the mellowest person's composure—he remained calm, almost steely in his determination not to lose control.

Twelve years later, that same characteristic would be on display for the world to see when, hours before the presidential

election, his grandmother Toot—the woman he often said had
been the most important person in his life when he was growing
up, whom he had flown to Hawaii to pay a deathbed visit to a
couple weeks earlier—died. While clearly emotionally shattered,
Obama somehow managed to pull himself together to deliver a
series of extremely powerful last-minute speeches in Florida and
Ohio, dabbing at his eyes to wipe away the tears and then getting
on with the business at hand. It was a bravura performance, similar, in many ways, to how John F. Kennedy handled the death of
his and Jackie's infant son, Patrick, in August 1963.

Time and again during the long election campaign, that steely
calm was on display for all to see. When Obama's team members
started flipping out in the face of, say, unfavorable poll numbers
or unfathomably bad economic data, he tended to remain calm,
the still center at the eye of the storm. Organizer friends from the
1980s recollect the only sign he ever gave of being ruffled was
smoking two Marlboros in a row instead of his usual single smoke.
Those rare moments they termed "two-cigarette situations." *Did
they ever see a three-cigarette situation?* Not once.[6] "I've never seen his
emotions fluctuate," fund-raiser Alan Solomont avers. "I've never
seen peaks and valleys. Bill Clinton was notorious for having a
temper, getting red in the face. You never see that with Barack,
even in private. This is a guy who's cool as a cucumber."

Obama was, many of his friends felt, someone who stayed
cool not just because he realized it played well, but because he had
spent the time doing what Charlie Halpern called "inner work";

he had put in the effort to understand his place in the world and out of that effort had developed a powerful sense of equanimity. To Halpern, the president came across as a man imbued with the kind of calm, or wisdom, developed by people over many years of meditative practice. It was a serenity, a wisdom built upon the ability to distinguish the truly important from the trivial, that Halpern usually associated more with the Dalai Lama, whom he knew, than with politicians. "It reminds me of the Kipling poem 'If,' " Harvard Law School friend Hill Harper says of Obama's even-keel temperament. "There's a line in there, 'If you can keep your head while others around you are losing theirs.' "

For Alan Dershowitz, this translated to "emotional intelligence": "He knows himself. He knows his strengths, knows his limitations, understands himself very well, and knows how the public reacts to him." Dershowitz, who is notoriously hard to impress, quotes a famous line by Supreme Court Justice Felix Frankfurter on Franklin Roosevelt. The president was, Frankfurter declared, a second-rate intellect with a first-rate temperament. Obama, says Dershowitz approvingly, has first-rate intelligence to go with his sterling temperament.

Erwin Hargrove, emeritus professor of political science at Vanderbilt University and author of *Effective Presidency,* puts it this way: "There's an inner serenity there that you don't find in too many politicians. Along with an ambition. It reminds me of Lincoln or FDR, both of whom combined serenity and ambition. But I don't detect any of the deep needs for attention, the insecurities that you find in Nixon or Lyndon Johnson. And I don't find any arrogance or hubris. I find a certain humility. Although he knows, as Lincoln did, that he's the smartest man in the room."

FLYING HIGH

At the nadir of the presidential campaign, with the GOP launching a full-court barrage of negative ads and with Obama's level of popular support seemingly stalled, the candidate convened a conference call with his national finance committee and all his top policy advisers. *You've got to go negative, you have to pay the GOP back in kind*, they told him. *You've got to play hardball.* Obama turned down the advice. *No,* he replied, *he would stay on message, keep pushing hope over fear.* A year earlier, at an intimate dinner with a few close friends and advisers in Chicago during the late summer of 2007, the candidate had received similar "go negative, go for the jugular" recommendations regarding Hillary Clinton. Then, too, politely but firmly, he declined the advice. "That's not the kind of campaign I run. We're going to do this the right way," one participant recalled him saying.[7]

It is a truism in the world of politics that campaigns reflect leaders. Hillary Clinton and John McCain's campaigns were full of chaos-fueled old-school operatives. Backstabbing was commonplace, and among campaign teams reporting to moody, nervous candidates, blame games were a dime a dozen. Obama's, by contrast, was cool, even if some of the key players, such as Rahm Emanuel, were notoriously hot-headed in other contexts. Participants on his hundreds of campaign conference calls recall that there was almost no swearing, hardly ever raised voices. "You know, everybody, I believe I have the kind of temperament necessary for the campaign and for the presidency. When things are very difficult, I stay steady," Colorado-based fund-raiser David Friedman recalls candidate Obama telling his national finance committee. "When things are really good, I stay steady." For Friedman, Obama was quite simply "hard-wired to have an even temperament."[8]

But that didn't mean he was unwilling to go out on a limb at times. A longtime poker player, Obama likes games of chance. "Barack has helped me loosen up and feel comfortable with taking risks," the New Yorker magazine quoted Michelle Obama telling photographer Mariana Cook in 1996.[9] He doesn't, though, take risks just to take risks, and he likes calculating the odds before he makes decisions. None of which is to imply that he's always averse to improvising, to cobbling together kludges to solve problems; but it does suggest that the risks he takes have generally been thought through from all angles first. As University of Southern California cultural historian Robin Kelley says, he's playing a Miles Davis album from the 1950s rather than the more anarchistic, free-form 1970s; Obama's relationship with risk is smooth, unjagged, easily pleasing to the ear.

When David Friedman came to D.C. to meet with Obama in early 2007 to strategize about a potential presidential bid, the two men talked in an utterly empty office building that Obama's people had rented as a possible Washington branch office for a campaign to be headquartered in Chicago. Obama knew the odds were long—after all, both Hillary Clinton and John Edwards had been amassing war chests and bringing in big-name supporters for months already—but even so, he liked his chances. "We are building the airplane as we taxi down the runway," Friedman recalled the candidate telling him. "Unlike other candidates, I did not know that I was running for the presidency six-plus months ago," Obama continued, perhaps just a touch disingenuously.

Of course, the plane flew. In fact, a more apropos analogy might be a rocket. Obama's campaign rapidly went into orbit. Over the nearly two years of campaigning, Obama edged out Hillary Clinton, a candidate who entered the race with an aura of inevitability surrounding her, and went on to outmaneuver and outperform the Republican candidate, John McCain, during the three-month sprint to November 4.

ONLY ONE THING BEATS A GOOD BASKETBALL GAME

Perhaps nothing exemplifies Obama's extraordinary ability to remain calm under pressure than his actions on Election Day itself. On the cusp of history, Obama retreated to a Chicago gym run by Tim McCrue, Michael Jordan's onetime trainer, to play basketball.[10]

Marty Nesbitt, a businessman in Chicago and Obama's closest friend, had brought together hoops-mates from the candidate's Hawaii, Harvard, Chicago, and D.C. days. As Obama, Nesbitt, and a handful of others flew back to Chicago from a morning event in Indiana, the Democrat and his friends strategized not about the election that day but about the basketball game, who would play with whom on the various teams. Including Obama, there were twenty-four men, all clad in jerseys specially made for the occasion. They were blue and white and had the words THAT ONE emblazoned on their fronts—a dismissive phrase John McCain had used in one of the presidential debates when referring to his Democratic opponent—along with a hand pointing to Obama's campaign symbol. It had been made to look like a basketball, twirling on an extended finger.

The friends divided up into four teams of six, and proceeded to play a series of round-robin games. "It was wonderful, because it really felt like we knew everything would be different," recalled Hill Harper, one of the players. Obama was "very relaxed. Just playing ball and hanging out, making jokes."

Midway through, Obama and his personal assistant, Reggie Love, bumped heads while chasing down a ball. Obama, joking, told his teammates, "Man, I'm going to go sit down. Maybe I should just rest, because I have a big night. It'd be best if I left here uninjured." Obama's team, according to one of his teammates, won one game and lost another; Barack was apparently a little tired but still managed to nail a few baskets. Then the two teams that had won both their preliminary games went on to play a "championship" game, enthusiastically cheered on from the bench by the presidential candidate and his team.

The game ended at five o'clock. Obama went to the Grand Hyatt Hotel to get a haircut and then headed out to dinner with his inner entourage. Shortly afterward, the poll results started coming in from the states on the east coast that were first to finish voting. Obama hadn't even had time to sit alone and ponder the momentous events at the epicenter of which he now resided. He hadn't allowed the magnitude of the day to overwhelm him.

CASE STUDY

TACKLING RACE HEAD-ON

In the months leading up to the election, three potential scandals involving friends or acquaintances threatened to derail Obama's presidential campaign: first there was his relationship with a corrupt Chicago real estate developer, Tony Rezko. Then there was the fact that he had worked on an education reform commission alongside Bill Ayers, a onetime Weather Underground leader from the early 1970s. Ayers's group, which represented the worst, most nihilistic side of Baby Boomer countercultural politics, had decided peaceful protests against the Vietnam War were ineffective, and so, in the name of revolution, they had embraced violence. Over the years, they claimed credit for a dozen bombings in their war against the American state. Finally, there was his decades-long association with the radical black preacher Reverend Jeremiah Wright, head of Trinity United Church of Christ.

Regarding Rezko and Ayers, Obama gambled that there wasn't enough dirt to stick to him. The Rezko connection was possibly sleazy—he had bought some real estate for below market price from Rezko—but not illegal. The less Obama addressed the story the harder it was for reporters and opponents to gain traction with it. Outside of Chicago, he figured, few people cared about Rezko.

True to form, Obama's strategy of nonengagement worked. The story became a sort of blowing-off-steam phenomenon for talk radio and Fox News shills, but most of the media quickly moved on.

As for Bill Ayers, the charges were pretty ludicrous to begin with—yes, Obama had worked on the Annenberg Challenge commission with Ayers, but then so had many other local notables. Obama had no trouble defusing the issue. He was, he pointed out, only eight years old when Ayers was alleged to have exploded his bombs, he knew the man in a setting at which many eminently moderate Republicans were also present, and he clearly didn't share Ayers's incendiary worldview. *Is this really the best you can throw at me?* Obama practically taunted his opponents.

But Jeremiah Wright, now that was a different story. Wright had been caught on tape soon after the 9/11 terrorist attacks shouting aloud "God damn America," saying that America's chickens were coming home to roost, and calling the country the U.S. of KKK A. He had accused the country's leadership of all sorts of national and international crimes. And in his sermons, played in endless loops on cable TV in the spring of 2008, he appeared to be weaving a web of inflammatory accusations against whites in general.

For Obama this was devastating, opening him up to charges that he was a closet "race man," someone who would put skin color above national loyalty. It was also more than a bit ironic: eight years earlier, he had been dealt a political thumping by Congressman Bobby Rush, an African American politician who, with the tacit blessing of many African American state senators in Springfield, had basically accused Obama of not being black enough.

Not black enough? Too black? Too angry? None of these charges jibed with Obama's sense of himself. Yet the "not black enough" charge had helped sink his Congressional ambitions in 2000. And now the "too black" charge had the potential to torpedo his presidential hopes.

Obama's gut instincts told him that he had to jump into the fray. After all, a large part of his electoral appeal, going back as far as his Harvard Law School days, came from his ability to "transcend race," to convince black and white alike that, as a biracial, multicultural man, he understood their hopes and fears and that he would be a president for all Americans. In fashioning his political message, he had learned from social justice organizers from decades past, men like Chicago's Father John Egan and Geno Baroni—a longtime organizer who ended up as an assistant secretary at the Department of Housing and Urban Development under President Jimmy Carter. These individuals had passionately believed that the issues of poverty they cared about transcended race and that the best way of organizing communities was to show poor people of all colors what they had in common.

"We have to deal not only with economic issues, but also with the cultural issue of America's diverse groups and its pluralism," Baroni told the audience at a January 1978 roundtable in Washington, D.C., sponsored by the American Enterprise Institute. "The only way that we will be able to deal with that so-called inevitable group conflict is to find convergent, joint issues between groups, and spend a lot of time on the problems of jobs, housing, education, and health."[1]

This foreshadowed Obama's credo perfectly. "One of the things I see organizing being able to do without getting directly involved in electoral politics," he had told an audience in 1990, "is plowing some soil so that when elections do come around and politicians come in with race baiting or demagoguery, enough work has been laid there so that—not that demagoguery is going to be ineffective, but that it will be less effective—there will be some counter voices to it."[2]

A year after this speech, that ability to cross racial lines allowed him to win election as president of the *Harvard Law Review*, beating out a field of eighteen other candidates. At a time of fairly pronounced racial tensions at Harvard—African American students were campaigning for the university to hire more minority faculty, conservative white students, many sympathetic to the newly formed Federalist Society, were mounting an intellectual assault on affirmative action, and tempers were flaring on all sides—Obama won the support both of black students and also of whites. Many of his supporters were fairly conservative, but, largely because of his already-developed listening skills, they believed that Obama, despite his liberal beliefs, would serve as a conciliator. (Ironically, Judson Miner, the attorney who hired Obama to work in his civil rights firm after he graduated from law school, first encountered Obama's name immediately after this election, when a small Chicago newspaper ran an error-strewn report claiming a local kid from the housing projects had just made good and gotten elected head of the *Harvard Law Review*.)[3]

So successful was Obama in befriending his opponents, remembered professor David Wilkins, that, twenty years later, when Republican Party operatives tried to dig up dirt on his *Law Review* tenure, they couldn't find any. Even the people who didn't like his politics liked and trusted him as an individual and felt that he had run the *Review* in an honest and above-board manner. It was, felt Wilkins, "a very important early indication of his remarkable ability to bridge divides."[4]

All these long years of perfecting the art of empathy had given Obama the ability to show, within the words of one speech or one passage from a book, that he understood black people's sense of citizenship deferred and also many white people's sense that with laws like affirmative action they were now getting the short end of the stick. "He's not coming out of a black nationalist bag or even an Afro-centric bag. He's coming out of something that's more like a rainbow, where he pays attention to every stripe of the rainbow," said Julianne Malveaux, president of Bennett College.

During the long campaign months of 2008, Malveaux had, at times, been highly critical of Obama for not more aggressively pushing African Americans' interests in his speeches. But she recognized the power of his inclusive rhetoric. "He clearly is a conciliator," she averred.[5]

And yet, notwithstanding all the conciliation work Obama and others had put in during the decade-plus in which Obama had been on the political stage, Wright's words now threatened to tear open all those divides and distrusts once more. Obama knew that after all his carefully laid groundwork to paint his candidacy as in some ways postracial, the words of the man he credited with bringing him to Christianity—a man who had presided over his and Michelle's wedding ceremony and whom he once told an interviewer represented "the best of what the black church has to offer"[6]—had the potential to tar him as an "angry black man." And he knew that if the narrative was about race, and that narrative wasn't on his terms, then he would probably lose. So, despite his advisers urging him to lie low—"this was," John Kupper said, "something to try to skate around without confronting directly"—he chose to intervene.

It was the biggest roll of the dice of his life, but he'd been left with little choice. This was a sword he would either fall on or be able to break off at the hilt. He knew it was a make-or-break moment for his entire candidacy. Even if the tapes had emerged too late for Hillary Clinton to secure a majority of the elected delegates, Wright's words had the potential to scare superdelegates into Clinton's corner. And even if that didn't happen, they could send candidate Obama into the presidential season a fatally wounded nominee.

At Obama's insistence, his campaign staff arranged for him to deliver a talk to America at the historic Constitution Center in Philadelphia, on March 18. Barack Obama pulled back on his campaign schedule and set to work personally crafting a speech that he knew had to both educate his audience about the nuances of black culture and also reassure voters of all colors that his would not be a sectarian administration.

He stayed up all night on the eve of the event, putting the finishing touches to a soaring speech, titled "A More Perfect Union"—which he e-mailed to David Axelrod only at six in the morning the day of the event—on the role of race in American life. Improbably, the speech would not just rescue his candidacy but actually make it far stronger.

Yes, he disagreed with many of Reverend Wright's positions, found some of them to be "profoundly distorted," "not only wrong but divisive," and "racially charged at a time when we need to come together." But, at the same time, Wright was also a tireless spokesperson for the poor and vulnerable, an apostle of hope when too many were steeped in despair.

In a passage that achieved near-instantaneous fame, Obama declared of his erstwhile pastor, "I can no more disown him than I can disown the black community. I can no more disown him than I can my white grandmother—a woman who helped raise me, a woman who sacrificed again and again for me, a woman who loves me as much as she loves anything in this world, but a woman who once confessed her fear of a black man who passed by her on the street, and who on more than one occasion has uttered racial or ethnic stereotypes that made me cringe. Those people are a part of me. And they are a part of America, this country that I love."

Throughout the more than half-hour speech, Obama kept coming back to economics, using a conversation about race to segue into something different; to a legacy of opportunity denied—young blacks increasingly channeled into prisons; or truncated—whites unable to achieve the middle-class status afforded their parents. He talked of the need for unity in the face of universal problems. "We want," he told his audience, "to talk about the crumbling schools that are stealing the future of black children and white children and Asian children and Hispanic children and Native American children . . . we want to talk about how the lines in the Emergency Room are filled with whites and blacks and Hispanics who do not have health care; who don't have the power on their own to overcome the special interests in Washington, but who can take them on if we do it together."

He came across, in Philadelphia as in so many other locales, as a great boxer, seemingly staggering backward, on the defensive, about to hit the ropes, only to sidestep his opponent and start moving forward again, regaining control of the ring one step at a time.

If there was a central theme to Obama's Philadelphia speech, it was the notion of empathy. His language convinced listeners that he could understand the grievances and hurts of generations of impoverished African Americans. He talked of African American neighborhoods of cities in which public services were sorely lacking; of banks redlining communities; of segregated schools, and prisons filled with young black men and women. And at the same time, his words assured those listening that he could equally understand the frustrations of whites who felt affirmative action and other social justice programs stood in the way of their own dreams. He spoke of economically vulnerable whites embittered by being "told to bus their children to a school across town," and angered "when they hear that an African American is getting an advantage in landing a good job or a spot in a good college because of an injustice that they themselves never committed."

The next day's *New York Times* reported glowingly that "Mr. Obama invoked the fundamental values of equality of opportunity, fairness, social justice. He confronted race head-on, then reached beyond it to talk sympathetically about the experiences of the white working class and the plight of workers stripped of jobs and pensions."[7]

Obama "learns with his head and his heart," observed Charlie Halpern, building on themes from his book *Making Waves and Riding the Currents: Activism and the Practice of Wisdom*. "He has an empathic mastery of history. And the learning he does is educating his heart as well as his head. He has put himself into the experience of the slave and the middle passage. I think he has put himself into the experience of Bakke, the white man [the plaintiff in a famous anti–affirmative action lawsuit]; white people who think black people are getting a free ride and they're getting screwed. And he does it in a way which is not just mastering the facts. That is a rare quality and it goes with his presence, the kind of attention he gives to the people who are talking with him. This is something that is very rare in American politics."[8]

There is a story, possibly apocryphal, of the pollsters who knocked on the door of a run-down house in rural Virginia in the autumn of 2008. The lady of the house answered. *Would you mind telling us who you are planning on voting for?* The pollsters enquired. *Oh,* said the lady, *I don't decide those things. My husband does.* The pollsters asked if she would mind finding out from her husband how they were planning on voting. *Honey!* she shouted, *these people here want to know who we're voting for.* From the upstairs of the house came this reply: *Tell 'em we're voting for the nigger!*

The anecdote is both horrific—in the rawness of the language, in the casual, unthinking layers of hatred revealed by the comment—and also strangely telling. Obama has the ability to win the support even of some people who have always been viscerally, casually racist. Should he save the American economy, it's more than likely that in 2012 that same man will be voting for Obama's reelection but without the racial epithets attached. To borrow a theme from Lincoln, Barack Obama has the potential to bring out the better angels in many, many Americans.

"I learned to slip back and forth between my black and white worlds," the young Obama wrote in *Dreams from My Father.* "Understanding that each possessed its own language and customs and structures of meaning, convinced that with a bit of translation on my part the two worlds would eventually cohere."[9]

There is, of course, a coda to the Jeremiah Wright story. Despite his sense of loyalty, Obama knows when to cut his losses. After Wright continued to go off-script even after the Philadelphia speech, making a series of bizarre, inflammatory, and self-aggrandizing statements, Obama publicly, and angrily, broke with his onetime mentor, during a speech in Hickory, North Carolina, on April 29th. "What became clear to me is that he was presenting a world view that contradicts who I am and what I stand for," Obama said. "And what I think particularly angered me was his suggestion somehow that my previous denunciations of his remarks were somehow political posturing. Anybody who knows me and anybody who knows what I'm about knows that I am about trying to bridge gaps and I see the commonality in all people."

It was a dramatic, much-reported event, the rarity of the candidate's emotional discomfort serving to underscore the seriousness of the rift. The subtext was clear: Wright was a loose cannon, a man more interested in the spotlight than in healing a nation's divides. Out of his mouth came *his* words, and his words alone—words that, candidate Obama now made clear, he had come to find distasteful in the extreme.

From then on, GOP attempts to link him to Wright—as with a barrage of attack ads in toss-up states like Pennsylvania in the waning days of the election campaign—failed to convert into tightening poll numbers. As with Rezko and Ayers, Wright had become a vanishing man. Yes, die-hard Republicans would raise his specter when warning the country that Obama was a Manchurian candidate; but independents would not, in any significant numbers, be swayed by Wright's purported demagoguery to vote against Obama.

Barack Obama had survived a potentially devastating episode. He had remained master of his own narrative.

CHAPTER SIX

CURIOSITY

Obama's writings and public speeches demonstrate an extraordinarily versatile, wide-ranging, intellectual mind. Like the Czech dissident-turned-national-leader Václav Havel, he is that rare political animal: a hard-nosed politician with a poet's aesthetic. "He's certainly the most blindingly talented guy I've ever met. He has just tremendous range, both his memory, his range of interests, his command of history," says Obama's ex–law firm colleague George Galland. "There are very few subjects in which Barack doesn't have a respectable fund of knowledge."[1]

When it comes to music, Obama is a jazz buff, likes R&B, grew up worshipping soul musicians, and enjoys some rap music. *Rolling Stone* magazine reported his musical loves include Stevie Wonder, Bob Dylan (the song "Maggie's Farm," the album *Blood on the Tracks*, in particular), Bruce Springsteen, the Rolling Stones, and even the Grateful Dead.[2] The enthusiasm is reciprocal; these musicians love Obama. Springsteen sang alongside a geriatric Pete Seeger at the preinauguration concert; Dylan, who has made a point of never endorsing political figures, went out of his way to tell audiences that Obama represented a massive change for the better—his "Times They Are a-Changin' " moment nearly a half-century on. Stevie Wonder gave a private performance at the White House shortly after the inauguration.

By all accounts, Obama's curiosity was nurtured in him by his mother, Stanley Ann. She was, he wrote in the 2004 preface to *Dreams from My Father*, defined by "her joy, her capacity for wonder."[3]

When the family lived in Jakarta, Indonesia, in the late 1960s, Ann taught English. Unlike most of the expat kids, who were enrolled in an exclusive American school, Barry attended local schools. He learned Indonesian and was kept up to speed on his English by lessons taught him by his mother in the small hours of the mornings. Day by day, he came face to face with an unfamiliar culture, learning to eat exotic foods—including, he writes in his memoirs, dog and snake—listening to the Islamic call to morning prayers, seeing up close the disease and poverty of a developing nation. Wherever Ann went, the kids went; they were allowed, and even expected, to take part in the grown-up conversations. The children were, Maya recalled, raised "in a manner different from a lot of American kids."[4]

In the early 1970s, as Ann and Lolo's marriage hit the skids, Ann made the decision to send Barry back to Hawaii to live with his grandparents. A year later she, too, returned, with the toddler Maya in tow. By then, Obama was already a scholarship student at the Punahou Academy, Hawaii's most elite school. Like the schools for children of privilege in the Northeastern states or Europe, Punahou had a mission: in addition to providing students a rounded, rigorous education, it hoped to inculcate in them a sense of noblesse oblige; those to whom much is given, the school's credo went, have a duty to give back. That credo was aimed at the wealthy elites who made up the great majority of the school's student body; it would also, however, have been taken to heart by Obama—a youngster from a nonprivileged background who had been given the chance of a lifetime to enjoy the fruits of a school like Punahou.

For the next several years, Ann and her two children lived in a small apartment in Honolulu. When Ann went on extended field trips in Africa and Asia, working with poor rural residents, sending reports back to international development agencies—Barack would live with her parents, Madelyn and Stanley Dunham, in their small condo near the beach. Periodically, Obama has written, the absence of his father, combined with the semi-absence of his mother, left him feeling like an "orphan." Yet at the same time, he clearly relished the breadth of experience and the range of interests his mother brought to their home.

When Obama's class graduated, on June 2, 1979, Punahou's then-president Roderick McPhee read aloud an old admonition, often attributed to Ralph Waldo Emerson but probably written by a woman named Bessie Stanley in the early twentieth century.[5] McPhee urged his students, as they went out into the world,

> *To laugh often and much;*
> *To win the respect of intelligent people and the affection of children;*
> *To earn the appreciation of honest critics and endure the betrayal of false friends;*
> *To appreciate beauty, to find the best in others;*
> *To leave the world a bit better, whether by a healthy child, a garden patch or a redeemed social condition;*
> *To know even one life has breathed easier because you have lived.*
> *This is to have succeeded.*

PUSHING THE ENVELOPE

After graduating from Punahou, Obama wanted to settle on the mainland, in a city with a more thriving intellectual scene than that which could be found in Honolulu. And so he enrolled at Occidental, a liberal arts college in Los Angeles, the quintessential city of personal reinvention.

In L.A., as the young student from Hawaii sought to broaden his horizons, he reported hanging out with "Marxist professors, and structural feminists and punk rock performance poets. We smoked cigarettes and wore leather jackets. At night, in the dorms, we discussed neocolonialism, Franz Fanon, Eurocentrism, and patriarchy."[6] That, to put it mildly, is a list of friends and intellectual references that you don't often hear an ambitious American politician bandy about. Fanon, born on the Caribbean island of Martinique but a man who spent much of his adult life in Algeria both before and after independence from France, wrote a book entitled *Wretched of the Earth* that praised violent revolts against not just colonial rulers but also colonial settlers in North Africa.

Obama attended Professor Roger Boesche's much-in-demand classes "American Political Thought" and "European Political Thought III: Nietzsche to the Present," in the latter reading books by Nietzsche such as *Beyond Good and Evil* and *Thus Spoke Zarathustra*. Boesche was a left-wing professor, but he generally kept his own politics out of classroom discussions. In his lectures, he referenced Karl Marx frequently—everyone at Occidental during those years, Boesche averred, seemed to be carrying around a copy of the Marx-Engels reader—but he also was quick to quote Thomas Jefferson and also the Federalist Papers. In addition to Nietzsche's works, for this class Obama would have read Sigmund Freud, sociologists such as Emile Durkheim and Max Weber, and Marxist scholars and revolutionary figures such as Lenin, Rosa Luxemburg, and Herbert Marcuse. He would also have read the existentialist Jean-Paul Sartre, as well as the philosopher Michel Foucault.[7]

Years later, when standing in for an ailing Ted Kennedy at a commencement address to Wesleyan students, Obama credited his time at Occidental and the classes he took there with spurring his interest in the world of ideas and also in the politics of social justice.

The young student's curiosity, however, wasn't limited to reading about ideas. It was also about wanting to experience new sensations. In Obama's teenage and early adult years, as he readily acknowledges, that curiosity led him to experiment with an array of drugs. He drank too much, developed an addiction to cigarettes, smoked pot, famously admits to having done "a little blow" (cocaine), and unapologetically describes his quest for new highs and chemical thrills. In *Dreams from My Father* he details how close he came to also trying heroin in the early 1980s; sitting in a room with an intravenous user, his arm primed to take the needle. And then, sensing the downward spiral such a choice would likely trigger, he pulled back.

That recognition of his own limits, of the need to calculate risk before embarking on a course of action, served as his saving grace, allowing him to avoid a life choice that all too easily could have veered into self-destruction. It presaged a future in which his curiosity would be more bounded. Without those boundaries, Michelle Robinson would, according to friends, likely never have let Obama into her life. "Both of them [Barack and Michelle Obama]," says Michelle's friend Elizabeth Hollander, a senior fellow at Tufts University's Tisch College of Citizenship and Public Service, "feel to whom much is given much is expected. But even that's wrong. It's not just that. One should lead a disciplined life. You get that sense from both of them. The stuff you gotta do, you gotta do. Even if it's hard. Those are the lessons he learned when his mother woke him up at four in the morning" to teach him English when they were living in Indonesia.[8] And they are the lessons Michelle learned while watching her disabled father struggle to work every day, to bring home the money that would eventually allow his two children to attend the best universities in the country. Barack stopped taking drugs and reduced his alcohol consumption to a beer or two, a glass or two of red wine, at a sitting. As he told it to *Rolling Stone* magazine,[9] he got his "ya-yas out" in school and college and moved on to better things. The main legacy of this experimentation seems to be an unconquered nicotine addiction—an occasional Marlboro cigarette, bummed from a friend, is the forty-fourth president's most visible vice.

Obama's description of his euphoriant dabblings is surprisingly frank. Thus, unlike Bill Clinton, who everyone knew had smoked pot back in the 1960s but who jumped through hoops to implausibly deny that he had inhaled, Obama, when asked, said something to the effect of "of course I inhaled. That was the point." The honesty is practically endearing. Almost everyone can relate to this, either through personal experience or through the experiences of children, cousins, or friends. The admissions of past illegal drug use end up coming across as sincere rather than seedy. As a result, when fellow Democrats tried to use his acknowledged actions against him in the primaries, and the GOP in the presidential campaign, the accusations fells on deaf ears. His opponents seemed surprised by this; after all, according to conventional political logic, after decades of tough-on-crime rhetoric raising the specter of a black man corrupted by the world of drugs ought to have shattered Obama's credibility. But Obama seemed to have read the public's shifting sentiments correctly. Quite simply, most voters weren't interested in the personal behavior of a young man being used to pass judgment against a mature adult a quarter century later. Obama's team of advisers, rather than rushing out press releases "clarifying" their candidate's position vis-à-vis drugs, simply ignored the issue. The tactic worked. Instead of becoming mountains standing in the way of electability, the drug allegations remained molehills.

COOL CATS, WHISKEY, AND LAUGHING AT VARMINTS

In his cool persona, many commentators have compared Barack Obama to jazz trumpet great Miles Davis, whose music, along with that of Thelonious Monk, Charlie Parker, and John Coltrane, the president deeply admires. But, says Robin Kelley,[10] the analogy isn't an easy one. Obama is far from Miles Davis the person—who was notoriously edgy, explosive, and unpredictable, his coolness always seeming to mask a just-beneath-the-surface violent rage. Rather than being like Davis himself, Obama is, argues Kelley, more like the man's *music* from the 1950s, from the *Birth of the Cool* years.

In Obama's personality, "there is no danger. On the contrary, there's nothing but safety. If anything, it's not Miles Davis the person, but it's Miles Davis the soundtrack. The soundtrack he carries with him is kind of blues," Kelley believes. The analogy extends to trumpeter Chet Baker's music, too; smooth, yearning. Obama, says Kelley, represents grace under fire. "There's a certain period of Miles's life from the fifties, early sixties, that brings the listener a sense of calm, and comfort, and even swing. There's no frivolity there. But it's really, really, cool." The thing about Miles Davis, says Kelley, was that "he always played the soundtrack of his time. I think that Obama, in some ways, his identification with Kennedy more so than Lincoln is extremely important. Because in some ways Kennedy was the perfect president for his time. It's the time of *cool*. Of American cool. The music became cool. Clothing style became cool. 'Cool' became the adjective of the day, in the midst of the Cold War. In some ways, what people find attractive about Obama is not that he is the hip-hop president but that he is Kennedy redux. He's a throwback to that time when people think things were much better, that life was better, and things would be OK. Because America was hegemonic. American cool has everything to do with that. The postwar American Empire, the American century. 'We are the most powerful nation on earth.' Obama in some ways has an investment in that idea, the American century."

It is an investment that emerges in myriad settings. When, for example, the Obamas were casting around for an interior designer to remodel the White House living quarters, they ended up choosing Michael Smith, a young designer from Los Angeles who specialized in creating airy classic American interiors using a mix of high-end materials and ultra-affordable ones. Not entirely Old World. Not entirely nouveau either. Rather, the designer's style represented a conscious, and quintessentially American, blending of oeuvres. Smith, whose elite client list included such luminaries as Steven Spielberg and media mogul Rupert Murdoch, was known to purchase goods from Target and Urban Outfitters as well as more selective boutiques, an eclectic shopping style similar to that reputedly utilized by Michelle Obama when putting together her wardrobe.

Whether in his reading preferences or his thinking about interior decor, Obama is an incarnation of that once-in-a-generation phenomenon: the intellectual president. In the late nineteenth century, President James Garfield, a professor of classical languages, was reputed to be able to write ambidextrously, one hand penning Latin while the other scribbled ancient Greek. In the early twentieth century, Teddy Roosevelt, one of only a handful of presidents to occupy the White House at a younger age than Obama, both wrote and read voraciously, oftentimes shaping major policy initiatives in response to books he had encountered. At least in part, the regulation of the meatpacking industry, for example, was a direct result of Roosevelt's fascination with muckraking journalist Upton Sinclair's book *The Jungle*. As a young man, Winston Churchill, arguably the consummate writer-politician of the twentieth century, modeled himself on Roosevelt, to the considerable annoyance of the older man. Woodrow Wilson, a few presidents later, was a highly talented political scientist, a PhD, and onetime president of Princeton University. In the early 1960s, John Kennedy similarly modeled himself as a man of ideas. Camelot, a term credited by insiders from that period to First Lady Jackie Kennedy, was more than a governing body of politically savvy technocrats; it was intended to conjure up images of bold thinkers, of *questers* after ideals.

"It was fun—because he was one of the more exciting people that you could be around," remembered Kennedy's long-time assistant and friend, Richard Donohue,[11] currently board vice chairman of the Kennedy Library. "He had a mind that was actually very alive and very catholic. In other words, you never knew what he was interested in. You would open the door, and he could start talking about baseball, politics, government. He could go from subject to subject quickly. His mind could flick from one thing to another instantly. He basically never forgot a conversation." In the 1990s, Donohue worked with Barack Obama on the board of Chicago's Joyce Foundation. As in Kennedy before him, in Obama Donohue saw a man of artistic temperament who was "smart as hell. There's some equivalency with him and Kennedy in terms of brain power. Kennedy was the smartest guy I ever met. Obama comes in a close second. He's very, very good. He can assimilate material with unbelievable alacrity. He'd not only absorb it, he could repeat it back. If you ever had given him information that turned out different, he was quick to note that."

While George W. Bush was widely criticized for being stunningly uncurious—Al Gore once said the thing that most disappointed him about the Bush presidency was the commander-in-chief's lack of intellectual engagement—Obama can reasonably lay claim to being one of the most ideas-driven presidents in America's history. "He's a voracious reader and he's got an insatiable curiosity," professor Douglas Brinkley asserts.[12] "The cut of his jib, we haven't seen anything like it since John Kennedy." He is, Brinkley adds, "a bit of an artist. I'm constantly amazed at how much he's read and how much he knows. Obama seems to read and it has effects on him. He's not a policy wonk, per se, just acquiring information. He allows information to flow in in an emotive way. This happens to very smart book-lovers."

In his memoirs, Obama describes arriving in Manhattan, following his decision to transfer from Occidental to Columbia University—he wanted to experience New York, as well as a hotter intellectual climate—and spending his first night sleeping in an alleyway after he failed to connect with the friend of a friend whose apartment he had arranged to sublet. Later he writes of living in dank, drafty apartments in New York, and of staying up into the small hours of the morning listening to Billie Holiday, drinking whiskey, smoking cigarettes on the fire escape. There's an almost Walt Whitmanesque or Jack Kerouac–like quality to his vision both of himself as a young man and of the city surrounding him. "More and more too, the old name absorbs into me Mannahatta, 'the place encircled by many swift tides and sparkling waters.' How fit a name for America's great democratic island city! The word itself, how beautiful! How aboriginal! How it seems to rise with tall spires, glistening in sunshine, with such New World atmosphere, vista and action!" Whitman wrote.[13]

New York is a city tailor-made for dreams, saturated with peoples and ideas from all over the world. It is, in short, a perfect fit for a young man of Obama's polyglot background and experiences. Obama would spend hours exploring his new city, soaking in the atmosphere and the sense of old worlds colliding and new ones emerging. "I spent a year walking from one end of Manhattan to the other," Obama wrote in *Dreams from My Father*. "Like a tourist, I watched the range of human possibility on display, trying to trace out my future in the lives of the people I saw."[14]

Once he graduated from Columbia and accepted a job as a community organizer, Chicago, home to such gritty authors as Nelson Algren and Studs Terkel, would come to assume that same role in his psyche. Reverend Alvin Love, one of Obama's oldest friends in the Windy City, recalls that there, too, Obama would spend hours walking through often rough streets, looking for churches at which he could meet with pastors and try to get them involved in his organizing efforts.[15] He was, and would remain, a big-city person. Years later, when he and a fellow state senator, Bill Haine, got into a friendly debate about the merits of making all-terrain vehicle drivers wear helmets, Obama supported the bill and Haine opposed it. Most ATV accidents, Haine said, were caused by the vehicles flipping rather than the drivers being thrown onto their heads. Moreover, he went on, his downstate constituents used ATVs to "chase varmints" off their farms, and it was too much for the state to demand they helmet up every time they saw a varmint. Obama started laughing so hard he couldn't stop. "Looking for varmints," he exclaimed, as he struggled to catch his breath. It sounded, to him, just as funny as could be. "He's a city guy," Haine explained. "He just thought it was a hoot."[16] The bill went down to defeat.

Read Obama—his memoirs, the essays he penned for little-known publications while a community organizer, the contributions he made to friends' books while a U.S. senator—and you're clearly reading the words of a thinker not wedded to a single, one-size-fits-all ideology. Instead, you are reading the words of a humanist, a man with the chaos of America's biggest cities jostling in his soul and the understanding that people can't be shoehorned into behaving as you want them to behave, committed to bettering the human condition but not to enforcing a political orthodoxy. Obama the writer, like Obama the politician, is a sampler; he takes good ideas from other thinkers while setting aside the accompanying ideological baggage. Perhaps that's why he is so enamored of non-gangsta hip-hop. It is, he told an interviewer for Black Entertainment Television in early 2008, smart and insightful music. Talking of artists such as Jay-Z and Kanye, Obama said that "the way that they can communicate a complex message in a very short space is remarkable."[17] While he is somewhat wary of hip-hop's materialist values, he recognizes its effectiveness in delivering a wide-ranging message to a large audience. The medium's sampling methods mesh perfectly with his political persona.

THE WORLD'S TOO COMPLEX FOR SOUND BITES

That persona developed over many years in Chicago, helped along by one man in particular. If anyone served as a mentor for Obama after he attained his law degree, it was Abner Mikva, a man who years earlier had been rebuffed by Obama when he had, sight unseen, offered him a U.S. Court of Appeals clerkship. A skilled legal mind, Mikva had served in the Illinois legislature as well as the U.S. House of Representatives. He had also worked a stint as White House counsel for Bill Clinton. By the mid-1990s, he was back in Chicago, teaching a legislative process class at the University of Chicago's law school.

While Mikva had been mildly surprised by Obama's long-distance rejection of his clerkship offer, when, a few years later, he met the young man, now a state senator and lecturer at the law school, he was captivated. Obama, he remembered, "was extremely well-read. He reads voraciously, or did back then. There was almost not a book you could talk about that he hadn't read. Political biography. History books. Current events. The law. He was teaching constitutional law at the time. I was teaching the legislative process. He was always fascinated by how the legislative process worked and how it fit into the constitution." For Mikva, the young man "just had all the skills. He was personable, he was smart, he was thoughtful, he was interested in all kinds of different things. Was eclectic. A lot of academics zero in on their specialty and you can't get them to talk about anything except their little territory. Barack was always very broad-gauged, was interested in everything, especially what you were doing. The university thought very highly of this."

Over the next several years, Mikva played senior-statesman adviser to the young protégé Obama. They would talk about what worked and what didn't work in Bill Clinton's presidency, how a man with a personal life so publicly flawed could nevertheless excel electorally. They would analyze why Harry Truman, a man of modest education, so successfully rose to the challenge of rebuilding postwar Europe and setting in place the cornerstones of American Cold War strategy. They would discuss Lincoln's cabinet choices, his approach to slavery, his maneuverings to save the Union. Obama understood, Mikva felt, "that particularly in government, people play a role far beyond their particular accomplishments." History was not made simply by padding one's résumé. As so many others had found before him, Mikva determined Obama to be extremely good at understanding complicated ideas.[18]

Obama understands the world to be dynamic, complex and ever changing, said one senior campaign adviser. "He didn't grow up with traditional frameworks. He is suspicious of dogma. It's his instinct to not start with some simplified construct or understanding of a problem."

The instinct to not reduce the world to sound bites makes for a complicated political vision and, equally, a pluralistic religious understanding. Obama is religious but not dogmatic; he's not the type of person to accept Biblical literalism, to be told exactly how to think about fundamental issues. "My religious faith is premised on some measure of doubt. That's why it's faith and not science. When I read scripture, I'm in a constant interpretation: what is God trying to say?" he told a New York City audience in 2004.[19] He likes reaching his own conclusions, believes in evolution, doesn't feel his religion precludes him from supporting a woman's right to choose when it comes to access to abortion. His faith is gentle, tolerant, and also political. It is influenced by liberation theology, by the heritage of the black church in America, and, to a degree, by religious thinkers such as Jim Cone, an African American theologian who taught at Union Seminary and in 1969 published the influential book *Black Theology and Black Power.* "Being black in America has very little to do with skin color," Cone wrote.[20] "To be black means that your heart, your soul, your mind, and your body are where the dispossessed are." For Cone, black theology was an emancipatory ideal; it was an affirmation of a black person's humanity.

Obama's faith is also ecumenical, borrowing not just from Christianity but from the world's other great faiths. He was clearly influenced as a boy by what he calls the "tolerant" version of Islam practiced in 1960s Indonesia.[21] He was also deeply moved by his reading of Mahatma Gandhi's autobiography and his teaching of a pacific form of Hinduism.

Obama, says his longtime friend Reverend Love, is less interested in Biblical minutiae than in the broad pictures painted by the authors of the Bible. "He may be more along the thought-for-thought lines than the word for word. What's the thought that they're trying to get across, and what's the intent? What is God saying with broad strokes, rather than trying to remember or recite every single word. Barack would be much more interested in knowing where to find the word in the Bible than being able to recite it simple chapter and verse." He isn't afraid to bring religious values to the table when he approaches policy problems, but won't let religious doctrine always dictate his policy solutions. Regarding access to abortion, for example, Love says that Obama refuses to think of pro-life and pro-choice positions as being at the opposite ends of a spectrum. Rather, he says, everyone ought to agree that it would be a good thing to reduce the number of abortions carried out in America. The question is, how best to do so? For Obama, passing legislation outlawing abortions would just drive the industry underground; by contrast, providing better education, better access to contraception, and so on, while keeping abortion legal, might actually more successfully achieve the desired effect.

Reverend Robert Jones says that for Obama denomination isn't important. "God's in the middle of the table, so to speak; and every religion is pointing to the center of the table. Every religion may not be pointing from the same direction; but they're all pointing to the center of the table."²² Jones, a long-time community organizer who used to pastor a church in southern Illinois and who helped introduce Obama to churches and communities in that part of the state when he was running for the U.S. Senate, recalls Obama visiting black churches, clapping with the choir, and "witness[ing] as anyone else would. He'd be fired up." Yet his friend wouldn't hesitate to diverge from some of the church's more conservative social and religious stances; he was, he and Jones would tell critics, running to be U.S. senator from Illinois, not U.S. minister.

WITHOUT IMAGINATION YOU CANNOT
LEAVE THE GROUND

When Obama was a boy, he recounted in *Dreams from My Father*, he visited a local library in Honolulu to search for his ancestral roots in Africa. He wanted to find, he reported, "my own magic kingdom, my own glorious birthright."[23] Later, when listening to Reverend Jeremiah Wright's sermon on the audacity of hope, he writes that it triggered in him images of "the stories of ordinary black people merging with the stories of David and Goliath, Moses and Pharaoh, the Christians in the lion's den, Ezekiel's field of dry bones. Those stories—of survival, and freedom, and hope—became our story, my story."[24]

Did it happen exactly that way? It doesn't matter. There's an implicit poetic license in much of *Dreams from My Father*. It's a memoir designed more to create impressions than as a faithful, literal, reproduction of events.

Muhammad Ali, one of Barack Obama's sporting heroes—a man whose photograph hung in his Senate office in Washington, D.C., and who attended the Democratic Party's national convention in Denver in 2008 to watch Obama being officially nominated as presidential candidate—used to say, "The man without an imagination has no wings; he cannot fly."[25]

Obama understands that basic need for imagination, the fact that man is, at heart, a storyteller. His all-time favorite television show is HBO's *The Wire*, a series on the gritty underside of Baltimore that critics routinely called Shakespearian in its dramatic arcs. (Shakespeare is also, apparently, one of his favorite authors.) Within the show, his favorite character was Omar, a lone-wolf stickup artist with a love of heisting money from bad guys, a mysterious man, impossible to pin down as to his exact motives.[26] Obama's favorite film is reputed to be *The Godfather*.[27] These are first and foremost great stories, myth-making American sagas.

In rural Kenya, searching for his ancestral roots, Obama visits his aging grandmother. She gives him his grandfather's Domestic Servant's Pocket Register, documentation he was issued while working as a servant to British colonialists in pre–World War Two days. She gives him a package of letters Barack Obama Sr. wrote to American universities requesting scholarships in the late 1950s and early 1960s.

Standing next to his father's and grandfather's graves, surrounded by mango trees and cornfields, Obama felt his surroundings closing in on him. "Until," he wrote in his memoirs, "I was left with only a series of mental images, Granny's stories come to life."[28]

Fragments, in the end, are what we use to weave the stories of our lives. The civil rights movement's leaders knew that part of their moral force lay in the fact that the civil rights movement itself had become a story. Myths could be fashioned out of it. Heroes could be created. The Obama campaign, in turn, knew that Barack Obama's life saga, told and retold again, could serve as a mobilizing agent in and of itself. His story was, they felt, strong enough to catalyze a movement not just around issues but around the persona of the presidential candidate. "Narrative is how we learn to exercise agency; narrative is all about choice—and choice under conditions of uncertainty," explained Marshall Ganz, the central figure behind the Camp Obama training sessions for thousands of young volunteers. "What the stories teach is how to handle conditions of agency. The 'how to handle' is not so much 'What's my tactic?' as it is 'How do I avoid fear? How do I be creative? How do I be hopeful?' Much more of an emotional content than a conceptual content. Narratives teach emotionally; they don't just teach conceptually." The stories Obama tells of his life, says Ganz, are designed to have audience members conclude, "I get where this guy is coming from."[29]

CHAPTER SEVEN

THINKING OUTSIDE THE BOX

Curious minds rarely hew to rigid worldviews. Maya Soetoro-Ng, Obama's younger sister, talks of the importance of empathy, the need to bring children up "in a way that is respectful but also nonauthoritarian." That way, she says, as adults they are more likely to be able to resist the pitfalls of unbridled nationalism, militarism, orders to commit acts of violence, and the like. In listening to her, you can practically hear the voice of her mother, the voice that helped mold Maya and her now-famous brother.

As a teacher, Maya has her high school students in Hawaii do an exercise that she calls the Doubting Game. *Take a belief you feel very strongly about, and dare to doubt it.* "You penetrate your own beliefs and force yourself to doubt everything." And then, you try to believe "beliefs that seem unimaginable to you," you learn to understand how people with whom you disagree think; you develop the capacity for empathy. It's a somewhat similar exercise to that practiced by the famous seventeenth-century philosopher

René Descartes. *Don't take anything for granted,* Descartes urged himself. *Challenge all your beliefs, and then, relying on induction, relying on knowledge accrued from experience, rebuild from the ground up.* Eventually the philosopher arrived at one thing he could not doubt: belief in his own existence. "I think, therefore I am," he declared. For Maya, encouraging her students to doubt everything didn't lead them into confusion but, ultimately, a sense of certainty. Out of the crucible of doubt would come "wisdom."[1]

Obama, too, approaches problems without locked-in-place ideological preconceptions. That is reflected by his choice of advisers, by his desire to hear all sides of an argument, and by his willingness to embrace unorthodox solutions to the problems of the moment, whether that means negotiating an ownership stake for the United Auto Workers in the Chrysler car company as a way of funding retirees' health benefits or reevaluating the methods by which America has conducted its War on Drugs since the early 1970s.

It is also reflected in his writings. In a review of his second book, *The Audacity of Hope,* the *New York Times*'s preeminent literary critic, Michiko Kakutani, wrote that *Dreams from My Father* was characterized by a "searching candor."[2] Like a successful novelist, Obama peppered his memoir with compelling dialogue; he brought alive not just the voices and idiosyncratic language of people he had interacted with over the years, but—at least as important—he re-created his own various voices; the angry young rebel seeking to understand his own racial identity, the earnest community organizer, the lawyer. He was, opined the novelist Zadie Smith, in a lecture that she gave at the New York Public Library a month after the 2008 election, "a genuinely many-voiced man."[3] Rachel Klayman, Obama's editor at Random House's Crown Publishing division, was deeply impressed by his ability to conjure up the voices of his central characters. His father, she felt, was portrayed as a "Shakespearian, tragic figure." The words of his older relatives in Kenya were replicated with an eye to the "oral tradition" of African narratives.[4] When he recorded a Books on Tape version of *Dreams*, Obama literally mimicked the voices of its characters.

His writings, especially the less guarded words of *Dreams from My Father*, hinted at someone with the sensibilities of, say, a James Baldwin, a Ralph Ellison, even a Jack Kerouac. They were poetic and questing, at times angry, at times simply astonished at the absurdities of life. And yet somehow, in addition to being literarily exciting, they also conveyed his political seriousness and his willingness to take on deep-rooted societal problems. Within American politics the combination was, at least in recent years, all but unprecedented. It allowed for a senior political figure to largely avoid clichés and to address complex policy questions using language that seemed real and emotions that came off as un-canned. He treated the members of his audiences as intelligent adults rather than putty to be shaped simply for his short-term political advantage. Hence the extraordinary sensation that his keynote speech to the 2004 Democratic National Convention caused. Here was someone who met the central condition of J. D. Salinger's epochal mid-century cultural challenge, laid down in

Catcher in the Rye: Was he a phony? The answer, if his words were to be believed, was a resounding "No."

For Douglas Brinkley, Obama's relationship to the written and spoken word opens up possibilities for dramatic cultural change. "Obama truly has this aesthetic, literary side to him. It's very refreshing to fellow writers. Because we recognize it, and we feel he's at least an auxiliary member of our tribe. He's extracting the wisdom from the literature and not just what's expedient. He's willing to be moved by the written word, poetry, song, painting. He hasn't written it off as being in the box of 'arts.' It all gets integrated into his daily life. There's an opportunity here for writers to actually play major roles in our public life for the first time since the sixties. Obama will read a good book or will ask to be informed about that book."[5]

Obama's careful reading feeds back into his own communicative skills. Even when he was a community organizer, applying for grants from the Woods Fund, board members recall that his proposals were superbly organized. He was, during these years, reading organizing tracts by men such as John McKnight, and also political biographies such as Bob Caro's masterful tome *The Power Broker*, on New York planner Robert Moses. Later, he would also read Caro's volumes on Lyndon Johnson. Reflecting both his writing skills and his intellectual references, Obama's weekly reports to the Gamaliel Foundation on his organizing experiences during these years, eight to ten pages in length, were reputedly gems of the genre, stylized observances on the often dry world of alliance building and grassroots education. How true that appraisal is, alas, will never be known: a few years before Obama was elected President, Greg Galuzzo, cofounder of Chicago's Gamaliel Foundation and one of the young Obama's organizing mentors, was clearing out a storage locker. Included in the items he threw away were boxes of old reports from organizers, among them Obama's contributions.[6]

RESPECT. EMPOWER. INCLUDE.

Hill Harper, a friend from Harvard, basketball buddy, and campaign surrogate, believes one of Obama's core strengths is that he is willing to work for people in whatever community setting they are located in; he will meet them and interact with them on their own terrain. He adheres to what people familiar with the ins and outs of various schools of community organizing call "relational organizing."

"The way to organize people is to create relationships between them, or better said, have them create relationships among themselves. And that in doing so, people learn about each other's hopes and fears, aspirations, values, issues," explains Jim Capraro, a Chicago-based progressive consultant with a long-standing working relationship with Obama. "Creating relationships is the most basic tenet, the most basic common denominator. Really strong community organizations are actually based on values, not issues. Issues come and go. That's not to say issues aren't important. Because working on issues is a means by which people can aspire to live their values. But working on issues isn't the only thing you can do. When you create relationships, people have common values. Barack Obama is nothing if not a relational human being. He listens well. That's the essence of a good relational organizer. What engages people to become involved in something and actually spend their own time, energy, influence, and money, is to feel heard, to actually feel listened to."[7]

Going all the way back to the nineteenth century, American social crusades such as the second Great Awakening, the abolitionist movement, and the early stirrings for woman suffrage had, argued Harvard's Marshall Ganz, "morally grounded claims that were both personally transformational and transformational of the world around, mobilized by highly dedicated teams of networks of organizers." Ganz taught his students how to weave stories of common interest from individual experiences; in his leadership classes, he emphasized the importance of narrative, of emotions, in engaging audiences. As head of the Obama campaign's Civic Engagement Subcommittee, he would use his teaching skills to help set up the Camp Obama training sessions for thousands of volunteers in 2007 and 2008.[8]

In December 2007, Obama and several other presidential hopefuls met with a roomful of community organizers in Iowa. Afterward, the candidate talked with Greg Galuzzo. "You know, Greg," he said. "Everywhere I go, people ask me how I learned to organize people and money the way I do." Then Obama stopped and laughed. "I tell people 'the Gamaliel Foundation, in Chicago, Illinois.' "[9]

Friends from his community organizer and civil rights law

days recall visiting him in Washington after he had won election to the U.S. Senate. Instead of the usual crowd of highly paid lobbyists one might expect to see in a new senator's office, they met consumer advocates, environmentalists, pro-choice spokespeople, and health-care activists. "I always saw him as an organizer in the Senate. He strategized with us," one of them explained.[10] "He told us where we [were] at in the Senate. He understood who should talk to who, who shouldn't talk to who. We saw him as a community organizer in the Senate. He used his community organizing skills to organize votes for us and help us strategize. He wasn't just a vote for us; he was a go-to guy for us."

Those traits carried over into the presidential election. "There's a remarkable, almost direct, translation of community organizing training activity that Marshall Ganz and others put together for Camp Obama. That wonderful curriculum is largely a telescoping of the training that organizers and leaders of community organizations are constantly getting," argues Jody Kretzmann, director of the Asset-Based Community Development Institute and a longtime Obama watcher. "'Respect. Empower. Include.' Those are core values for community organizers and were reflected in the field operation of the campaign."[11] At field headquarters all over the country, those three words were stuck on walls. In its capacity to energize, the slogan was to the Obama campaign volunteers what "It's the economy, stupid" had been for Bill Clinton's campaign back in 1992.

"In helping a group of housewives sit across the negotiating table with the mayor of America's third largest city and hold their own, or a retired steelworker stand before a TV camera and give voice to the dreams he has for his grandchild's future, one discovers the most significant and satisfying contribution organizing can make," a young and still unknown Obama wrote in 1990.[12] "In return, organizing teaches as nothing else does the beauty and strength of everyday people."

SHOOTING HOOPS IN THE PRISON YARD

Back in law school, Hill Harper was involved in the Black Students Association. He received a letter from a prisoner in the maximum security prison of Walpole, located halfway between Boston and Providence, Rhode Island. *Why weren't the black attorneys-in-training more engaged in finding out about prison conditions, about the lives that prisoners, many of whom were African American, led?* Harper's correspondent asked. The letter struck a nerve. Why *didn't* they visit prisons more often? Harper questioned himself. He sent a letter back asking if the prisoners would be interested in a game of pickup basketball with the Harvard guys. They were. He contacted the warden and inquired as to whether it would be possible to bring in a team of Ivy Leaguers to play his prisoners. The warden said such a thing had never been done before; then he thought about it, said he guessed it would be OK, and invited Harper to come on down to his facility. It wasn't exactly Johnnie Cash at Folsom Prison, but it *was* something novel.[13]

Harper rounded up four of his friends he viewed as being particularly strong players and convinced them to visit the prison with him. Barack Obama was among them. They got there, were ushered into a briefing room, and were told that the guards didn't walk in the yard with the prisoners; that if there were a riot, or the Harvard kids were attacked, they needed to make their way to predesignated corner areas, places toward which the officers on the watch towers above wouldn't shoot. *Were they sure they wanted to do this?* The warden asked again. The law school team was sure. Obama, the oldest among them, never flinched.

To hear Harper tell it, Obama spent the game guarded by a double-murderer. He wasn't a bit intimidated by the experience, though Harper—one of Obama's official speaker surrogates during the long, grueling, presidential campaign—jokes that Obama was notching up a fair number of points until he bothered to ask what the man guarding him was in for; when he found out it was for murder, he immediately stopped sinking baskets. *That's* judgment, Harper would joke to the crowds. And then, of course, he would quickly reassure them that he was just having some fun.

Being prepared to venture into uncharted territory, being willing to think outside the box, these were among Obama's most powerful inner strengths. That's what he was doing when he visited Rick Warren's Saddleback Church in the southern California town of Lake Forest and defended, in the most conciliatory terms possible, his pro-choice beliefs to a group of staunch evangelicals. "I believe in Roe versus Wade," the candidate averred. "Not because I'm pro-abortion but because ultimately I don't think women make these decisions casually. I think they wrestle with these things in profound ways, in consultation with their pastors or their spouses or their doctors and their family members." The goal, Obama stated, should be working out common ground, finding ways to reduce the numbers of abortions performed in America each year. "Are there ways that we can work together to reduce the number of unwanted pregnancies so that we actually are reducing the sense that women are seeking out abortions?"[14] In subtly changing the terms of the debate, he was able to engage with an audience that traditional Democrats had shied away from for decades.

Thinking outside the box: That's what he was doing, during the presidential election, when he decided to campaign hard in states like Indiana, North Carolina, and Virginia. No Democratic presidential candidate had won Indiana and Virginia since Lyndon Johnson's landslide victory over Barry Goldwater in 1964. None had won North Carolina since Jimmy Carter in 1976. Think according to old metrics, and there was nothing to suggest that a liberal black man in 2008 would break this string of losses. Obama, however, believed the old voting blocs were breaking down, and that these states were ripe for turning.

Thinking outside the box: that was the challenge he laid down to the Democratic Party's faithful at their convention in 2004, when he declared, "There is not a liberal America and a conservative America; there is the United States of America. There is not a black America and white America and Latino America and Asian America; there's the United States of America."

That was also what he had been doing back in his organizing

days when he talked with older men, like Northwestern University professor John McKnight, about the limits of Saul Alinsky's organizing strategies. Alinsky was the Godfather of the community organizing world, but he believed mainly in confrontation rather than compromise, in raucous demonstrations rather than mediation. For Obama, Alinsky's methodology encouraged people to think about their grievances rather than their hopes. Sure, Alinsky had attained prophet status among progressives of a certain age, but that didn't mean he'd gotten everything exactly right. During community organizing training sessions, Obama would have been asked to draw up two lists. The first delineated the characteristics of the world as it is; the second, the world as he, the organizer, would like it to be. For Alinsky, the former would never morph into the latter. For Obama, by contrast, that was the Holy Grail: laying down a challenge to take the world as you find it and turn it into something more approximating your ideals. "It begins on street corners and front porches," he told an audience in San Antonio on the evening of the Texas primary. "In living rooms and meeting halls with ordinary Americans who see the world as it is and realize that we have it within our power to remake the world as it should be."

Obama learned from the past, but he wasn't willing to be constrained by it. He had, after all, been thinking outside the box pretty much all his life. How could he not, given his heritage? He was a mixed-race child at a time when miscegenation—"The word is humpbacked, ugly, portending a monstrous outcome," Obama wrote in *Dreams from My Father*[15]—was still considered scandalous, was illegal in nineteen of the fifty states in the union. Quite literally, Obama's very existence was the result of Stanley Ann Dunham and Barack Obama Sr.'s ability to think outside their respective boxes. "In many parts of the South, my father could have been strung up from a tree for merely looking at my mother the wrong way; in the most sophisticated of northern cities, the hostile stares, the whispers, might have driven a woman in my mother's predicament into a back-alley abortion," Obama's memoirs continued.[16] That's quite a birth burden for a person to carry around with him.

In Chicago, Obama went into community organizing in part hoping to re-create in his own life the sense of idealism that had brought his parents together two decades earlier.[17] Recently graduated from Columbia University, he started working what fellow-organizer and gang intervention expert Al Kindle termed "the mean streets of Chicago." Kindle and the older, more street-smart activists watched Obama's back, talked to gang members so they wouldn't hassle him when he went onto their turf to mobilize people around, say, asbestos removal from a public housing project, helped build bonds of trust with neighborhood residents. "While he was in Chicago, we tried as best we could to educate him on the intricacies of our community. We had relationships. We introduced him to those relationships. Some of those mothers of the community. We had worked with them through the campaigns of Harold Washington, the fights of the sixties. He was new to the community. But *our* trust in him allowed people to put *their* trust in him. He came from the perspective in which he was trying to help. He was a young guy, trying to get started, who had an interest in trying to get something done. We'd always pledged we would help any young African American who was willing to lead in a new direction. We were looking for new leadership—to train and to promote."

Kindle felt that the newcomer "was a young guy on several levels. Age. His inexperience to the mean streets, the rough and tumble ways of Chicago, which in some ways is not like anywhere else in the world. There were always people who felt that . . . 'How does this young, educated guy come into the neighborhood?' There was always some of that. Resentment. Then of course there were people who wanted to know, 'Is this guy here to work with us or he is here just to report? What's his role?' We let people know, 'He's OK. Yes, he educated, but he's also OK. He's not been sent by the enemy.' In our community we want to know who sent you, and why. 'Why are you being sent and what's your mission? What are you here for?' Till they know who sent you and why, you get nowhere."

Obama managed to gain the community's trust. Soon, the older women were trying to fatten the skinny guy up, giving him plates heaped with greens and fried chicken, baking him cookies, whenever he visited their homes and community centers. "They began to adopt him. Particularly the residents in public housing," Kindle recalls. "They was impressed with him, the way in which he carried himself, and his thorough, detailed knowledge of the issues he was working around."[18] Obama would pick at the food, but generally not eat too much. For Obama, the big meal of the day was breakfast, often eaten at Valoi's diner, in Hyde Park. Come lunchtime, remembered fellow-organizer Linda Randle,[19] he preferred a good salad.

MAKING DREAMS COME TRUE

In 1991, after serving as president of the *Harvard Law Review*, Obama graduated magna cum laude from the law school. In a class of more than five hundred, all of whom were being groomed to assume top positions in American society, he had emerged among the top handful. *The cream of the cream.* (The only degree that would have topped it was summa cum laude, and no students in Obama's year or in the years immediately prior to Obama attained that rarified honor.) And lest anyone think that he'd been dealt with charitably because of the color of his skin, that he was somehow simply an affirmative-action creation—a claim that is, however unfairly, often leveled against high-achieving African American students—Harvard's grading system nipped such suspicions in the bud: students' papers at the Harvard Law School are graded anonymously, by student number rather than name. In awarding his work top grades, his professors had no idea they were reading papers by one Barack Hussein Obama.

With the magna cum laude in hand, a steady chorus of advisers told him to go for a Supreme Court clerkship or, at the very least, to allow a top corporate law firm to hire him on. *Do that,* he was told, *and the world is your oyster.* Abner Mikva, who at the time was serving as chief judge of the U.S. Court of Appeals in

Washington, D.C., sent an emissary his way specifically asking if Obama would clerk for him.[20]

Obama didn't think these were such good ideas. He had things he wanted to say, ideals he wanted to act on. He'd been approached about writing a volume of memoirs; he was being asked to lead a massive voter registration organizing effort in Illinois; and among the hundreds of calls he had gotten from law firms around the country, he was particularly intrigued by one from a small civil rights firm in Chicago, the city with which he had fallen in love and in which lived Michelle Robinson, with whom he was also smitten. He had phoned the lawyer back, left a message with his young daughter—*Daddy, someone with a funny name phoned for you,* Judson Miner later recalled his daughter saying—and, when he was next in Chicago, had talked with him over an extended lunch at a small restaurant near the office. Years earlier, Miner had been corporation counsel for the city of Chicago under Mayor Harold Washington. Then-Senate hopeful Carol Moseley Braun had once worked for Miner. His firm was well connected within the intimate world of progressive Chicago politics. Obama was intrigued.

The law school graduate was no longer a community organizer, but the values behind the organizing continued to animate him: he wanted to work with people and communities, and he wanted to weave narratives of empowerment. Abner Mikva's emissary returned to D.C. She told the judge that Obama had said thanks but no thanks. He wanted to work in the world of politics.

Back in Cambridge, faculty members close to Obama weren't surprised. They had long suspected that for him law would be a stepping stone to bigger things. He was, observed Professor Laurence Tribe, who had hired Obama as his principal research assistant in March 1989, "exceptionally brilliant, centered, mature, inquisitive, and pragmatic." Tribe felt the young man's "writing was concise and lucid and the power of his intellect was unmistakable."[21] He was, in short, born for politics. What Tribe saw in the late 1980s he saw again nearly two decades later when his protégé climbed to the pinnacles of power. He was using "remarkable analytical abilities to dissect and recombine policy options and political strategies."

Chris Edley, too, always saw Obama as something of a "drive-through" lawyer. "It's difficult as a private lawyer to shape your own agenda, as opposed to championing the interests of the clients who happen to come your way," says Edley. "With the talent that Barack has for envisioning social change, confining himself to the tools of a practicing lawyer would have been frustrating. He's got a lot more in his tool chest than that. He came to law school with a personal efficacy that he must have known couldn't be contained within the conventional role of a lawyer. He came to law school having already had powerful experiences of helping people, and he clearly came to law school because he was looking for tools that would allow him to help people on a grander scale. And once you start thinking like that you have to think beyond the conventional roles of the practicing lawyer."

In *World of Our Fathers*, the author Irving Howe quotes an early-twentieth-century immigrant as describing the United

States of America as being "in everybody's mouth. Businessmen talked of it over their accounts; the market women made up their quarrels that they might discuss it from stall to stall; people who had relatives in the famous land went around reading their letters for the enlightenment of less fortunate folk."[22] It was, the migrant continued, viewed as being a "magic land."

Of course, it almost goes without saying that the reality was never as smooth as the Dream itself. Most obviously, slavery and the segregated, unequal legacy it left in its wake were glaring limits to the Dream's universality. America's "peculiar institution" left a heritage so cruel and brutal that, for large swaths of the country's population, the soaring language of the Constitution appeared but a vicious mockery. That wellspring of heartache was spoken to in Martin Luther King's declaration that America had bounced a check when it came to including African Americans within the broad scope of the Dream. Less poetically, with less faith in the possibility for change, decades later it was spoken to also in the bitter words, shown in endless loops on cable television in the spring of 2008, uttered by Obama's pastor, Jeremiah Wright.

Over the centuries, the economic exploitation of America's poor, of all colors and from all corners of the globe, has also been an extraordinary obstacle to the realization of America's full, inclusive, democratic potential. The victims of the early-twentieth-century Triangle Shirtwaist Fire, female sweatshop workers locked inside a burning building in lower Manhattan; the impoverished sharecroppers of the pre–World War II South; the big-box store workers of our time forced to work extra hours off the clock to help store managers meet company profit requirements, all share the fate of living—and in some cases dying—a mangled version of the American story of promise and opportunity. So, too, do the two hundred-plus workers at the Republic Windows and Doors factory in Chicago who occupied their place of work in mid-December 2008, when banks refused to extend the company's lines of credit and the owners responded by trying to close the factory and summarily fire the workers. President-elect Obama declared his support for the workers and urged the company to pay them proper severance pay.

For all the extreme flaws, though, for many hundreds of millions, both in America and overseas, the words "American Dream" remained a symbol over the generations, an aspirational phrase representing hope, progress, and, above all, possibility. Obama wanted to take that sense of possibility and imagine what the United States *could* be rather than be satisfied with what it was. "I know my country has not perfected itself," the Democratic nominee-apparent for the presidency told a crowd of hundreds of thousands of Germans who had turned out to see him speak in Berlin, on July 24, 2008. "At times, we've struggled to keep the promise of liberty and equality for all of our people. We've made our share of mistakes, and there are times when our actions around the world have not lived up to our best intentions. But I also know how much I love America. I know that for more than two centuries, we have strived—at great cost and great sacrifice— to form a more perfect union; to seek, with other nations, a more hopeful world."

Obama's particular talent here, like Martin Luther King's before him, was to hold a mirror up to America, to get it to feel that it could, and indeed *had to*, do better when it came to race relations and, more generally, to social division. In the communal access to Obama's story, in his framing of his own saga as emblematic of everything hopeful in the American story, millions of Americans whose ancestors had lived as slaves finally could feel they had achieved full citizenship, more than 140 years after the Civil War's conclusion. Millions of others who took it for granted that the country's leaders had never listened to them before could feel a new sense of inclusion in the broader American community.

Obama wasn't an aesthete; having worked in depressed communities, he didn't glamorize poverty, and he had no desire to go through life poor. But nor did he intend to structure his career solely around promises of high salaries and bonuses. In 2005 he would tell a class of graduating university students in Illinois that "focusing your life solely on making a buck shows a poverty of ambition. It asks too little of yourself. You need to take up the challenges that we face as a nation and make them your own."[23]

EYES ON THE PRIZE

How to take up those challenges, though, was the great question. Depending on whom you talk to, Obama is either a pragmatist in the garb of an idealist or an idealist hiding behind a mantle of pragmatism. He is either a hard-edged dreamer or a subtle master of the fine art of realpolitik. The one thing most everyone agrees on is that Obama is hard to categorize.

He is instinctually a free trader, yet he clearly sympathizes with trade union critiques of NAFTA and the other trade agreements that largely shape America's role within the global economy. During the primary season, however, foreign policy adviser Samantha Powers, author of the book *A Problem From Hell: America and the Age of Genocide*, got caught telling Canadian officials that Obama's critiques of NAFTA were unlikely to result in significant changes to the trade agreement. He is an opponent of the war in Iraq, yet during the presidential election campaign, and in the first months of his presidency, showed himself to be something of a hawk on Afghanistan and Pakistan. He believes in multilateralism, yet recognizes America is the only country with a strong enough military to, for example, push for a just peace in the bloody conflict in Sudan's Darfur region or tackle piracy in the coastal waters off Somalia. He is willing to go outside his comfort zone, to venture into danger zones, in diplomacy, as witnessed by his much-debated statement during the election season that he would be prepared to meet with the leaders of countries such as Iran and North Korea to try to find common ground. John McCain taunted him for this, but the Democrat stood his ground. There was, he argued, no point in talking with only one's friends. On the other hand, during those same weeks, he carved out a far tougher line toward Pakistan than did the otherwise hawkish Bush administration or, for that matter, McCain. He has long favored universal health care, yet during the primary season, wary of alienating powerful lobbies such as the insurance industry, adopted a set of proposals more modest in their aims than those crafted by Hillary Clinton and John Edwards. He is a firm opponent of the notion that America has the right to torture terrorism-suspect detainees in certain circumstances; but in his first weeks in power, even as he prepared to release the infamous "torture memos" detailing how his predecessor's administration approved techniques such as waterboarding, his legal team accepted specific, extraordinary-case exemptions to the general rule that the limits imposed on interrogations by military manuals must always be adhered to by the CIA.

George W. Bush was, in many ways, a prisoner of conservative talk radio; his coalition was too dependent on the goodwill of people like Rush Limbaugh for him to want to risk their wrath too often. Obama's equivalent to talk radio is the liberal blogosphere, the cyberspace of Daily Kos and the Huffington Post. They animate his base and cheerlead (and sometimes carp) from the sidelines. Yet Obama has made clear on several occasions his willingness to stand up to left-leaning blogs when the need arises. Indeed, in mid-January 2009, as he prepared to assume the presidency, he convened a meeting not with liberal bloggers but with a coterie of conservative bloggers and commentators. The message was clear: *Don't try to pin me down. Don't mistake me for being two-dimensional.* Indeed, read Obama's campaign book *Change We Can Believe In*, and one can see that he faults Bush not so much for being a conservative as for being unable to change course in response to new situations. "These past eight years," he writes, "will be remembered for their rigid and ideological adherence to discredited ideas."[24]

If George W. Bush represented a nadir, it was a nadir created more by a blinkered way of doing politics than by the ideology of conservatism per se. Obama's clear distaste for Bush seems to have at least as much to do with *how* he governed than with the values that animated him; by contrast, he oftentimes expresses admiration for Ronald Reagan's style of governance. For despite his conservative leanings, in many ways Reagan was a realist, he was flexible. Rigidity, for Obama, is a far greater sin than conservatism.

"Yes We Can" and "We are the ones" are more than just mantras, or vague intimations of change, in this context. Rather they are shorthand for a whole set of visions about what a community, of whatever size, can do if it acts with a collective spirit. "I don't think you can really exaggerate the importance of his being involved in a rich organizing experience that was developing for a new period a politics that didn't think of people in categories or ideological terms," Harry Boyte suggests. "It's a very rich way of looking at people. It's a new civic politics." Where traditional technocrats and skilled professionals "learn to see people and communities in terms of their deficiencies, and not their capacities or assets," explains Boyte, organizers believe in encouraging a sense of possibility among ordinary people.[25]

Modern politicians, Boyte says, are usually "mobilizers," their world a cloistered one dominated by special interests and highly paid consultants. Obama, in contrast, is an organizer politician. And many of the people he brought into his campaign, from Boyte himself, who worked on the campaign's Civic Engagement Group, to Harvard's Marshall Ganz, are people who cut their teeth doing community organizing work in the 1960s and 1970s. One of Ganz's ex-students, a young woman named Buffie Wicks, was hired as a campaign director for fourteen western states, with a mission to integrate organizing tools into the campaign. Another of Ganz's protégés, Jeremy Bird, was appointed field director for the entire campaign. Government, these people believed, should serve as a catalyst, its actions, like many of those carried out by New Dealers in the 1930s, intended to produce magnifier effects throughout society.

In April 2008, as the presidential primary season neared its climax, Boyte drafted a speech for Obama titled "The Work of Citizenship": "When politicians think of voters simply as needy victims or as consumers of government services they are focusing only on one third of Abraham Lincoln's famous formulation at Gettysburg. They are pretending that government does things only *for* the people. They are forgetting Lincoln's full phrase, 'government of the people, by the people, for the people.'" Later in the speech, the candidate declared, "The genius of America comes when we remember this lesson, that we are a producer democracy, not a consumer democracy. 'We the people' is a nation of citizens, not a nation of customers."

IF YOU TALK STRAIGHT, PEOPLE LISTEN

In the late spring of 2008, gas prices soared past four dollars a gallon. To Americans, used to paying less than half that, this was catastrophic. Weekly budgets were being busted wide open; people were racking up huge debts just to be able to buy gas to drive to work.

Sensing an opportunity to make political hay, Hillary Clinton and John McCain came out in favor of a "gas tax holiday." It was a gimmick—prevent states from collecting a few cents per gallon in gas taxes and sell yourself to the electorate as working to reduce oil prices. But it was a gimmick that, according to most calculi, ought to have had legs.

Obama knew the proposal was a snow job; and he knew it did nothing to really solve America's energy crisis. It was as laughable as the Republican slogan used later in the campaign, after Alaska governor Sarah Palin's nomination as vice-presidential candidate, to "Drill, baby, drill." But he also knew that energy prices had never been so high and that any politician who stood in the way of even temporary relief risked being labeled a spoiler. In a world of sound-bite, focus group–driven politics, this could prove fatal.

Had he been Bill Clinton, urged to "triangulate" by political consultant Dick Morris, he would probably have tried to split the difference, perhaps advocating a partial tax holiday. Instead, he decided to take a chance, to address the American electorate as adults and tell them the hard truth. The tax holiday was, he argued, a bad idea. It would rob state governments of much-needed revenue, used to invest in infrastructure projects, and in putting only a few dimes or quarters back into drivers' hands each time they filled up, it wouldn't really help individuals plug the holes in their pocketbooks created by the energy crunch. He was thinking outside the gimmick-is-good political constructs that had dominated politics for decades. He was gambling that his audience no longer wanted to be pandered to, that they were yearning for leaders who would address them respectfully, grown-ups talking to grown-ups.

Obama's pollsters believed he was taking a "bold stand" that wouldn't necessarily go over well with voters. (In the world of political consultancy, words like "bold" and "brave" are often coded ways of saying "stupid" or "politically suicidal.") But when they polled people *after* Obama had come out against the tax holiday, it turned out that more people agreed with the candidate's stance than disagreed.

For Obama, eschewing the easy, tried-and-tested paths to popularity was nothing new. As far back as 1995, when he was just a local lawyer trying to make his way to the state legislature in Springfield, the candidate asked *Chicago Reader* reporter Hank de Zutter, "What if a politician were to see his job as that of an organizer, as part teacher and part advocate, one who does not sell voters short but who educates them about the real choices before them?"[26]

Throughout the presidential campaign, one adviser remembered, he kept urging his people to "think outside the box." *Don't just think about immediate problems*, he told his teams, *but ask yourself what you want the United States to be in twenty-five years; then ask your-self what it will have to look like in ten years in order to reach that goal; then ask yourself what it ought to look like in five years.* "He's a consummate educator," the adviser said. As a law school lecturer, he viewed the classroom as a place for intellectual give-and-take between students and lecturer; similarly, at a town hall meeting, rather than fall back on tired clichés and canned responses, he actually tried to think through the questions the audience asked of him. "He has," the adviser argued, "an eagerness to live in the moment and think in the moment" in such settings, a confidence in his ability to think on his feet. "He views politics as an educational enterprise. Everything in your life to some degree has the potential to teach you something. This is a keen observer of human nature."

In his first days in office, many pundits advised Obama not to bite off more than he could chew as a new president. *Pick one or two reforms, and concentrate on them.* Obama didn't agree. A crisis of the magnitude faced by America in early 2009, he believed, presented opportunities for wholesale reform. The public would tolerate huge government borrowing and deficit spending of an order that in normal times would be impossible to sustain. *Use the crisis,* he believed. *Think holistically.* Instead of piecemeal changes, the new administration pushed for huge changes to the country's health-care system, expanded unemployment insurance, massive federal spending on infrastructure projects—including, in a nod to Roosevelt's rural electrification program, bringing broadband Internet access to remote rural areas—unprecedented investments in green technology, changes to the tax codes, and a new regulatory structure for financial institutions.

The nation's forty-fourth president wasn't interested in a few infield singles. Eighteen years after winning his first election, at the *Harvard Law Review,* Barack Obama was swinging for the fences.

CHAPTER EIGHT

THE SMOOTH POLITICIAN

In 2000, Harvard Law School organized a reunion for all the school's African American graduates. David Wilkins was charged with putting together a panel for people who were serving in public office. He recommended Obama for the panel. *Obama?* his co-organizers asked, incredulous. *He's only a state senator. He's a nobody.* "No," Wilkins riposted confidently, "he's the future."[1]

That same year, a near-penniless Obama couldn't even get a floor pass to the Democratic Party's national convention in Los Angeles. Nine years later, he would be the most powerful man on earth.

While his rhetoric is centered on a somewhat hard-to-pin-down mantra of "change," underneath the utopian veneer is a hard-edged politician. That doesn't mean the idealism isn't real; rather it means that it is carefully tempered, fine-tuned to seduce as many as possible while alienating as few as possible. Time and again, the combination of idealism and realpolitik has proven to be an extremely potent vote winner.

At the University of Chicago, Douglas Baird approached his colleague, then–state senator Obama, in 2002, and asked him his opinion as to whether he should endorse a particular candidate for Illinois governor. Baird had already asked this question of Abner Mikva, and Mikva had told him, in no uncertain terms, *not* to endorse a man who was sure to lose.[2] Obama's answer was different. First, he said, as if this might affect Baird's decision, he himself *wasn't* running for governor—in response to which, Baird acknowledged, "my jaw may have dropped," because Baird hadn't asked Obama that question; second, like Mikva, he agreed that the man was going to lose. *But,* he added, the guy was clearly the best candidate, and that ought to count for something. Baird decided to give his endorsement; it was, for him, an example of how Obama was ambitious, pragmatic, and yet at the same time endearingly idealistic, a balance of traits that rendered him somewhat comparable to Bobby Kennedy. Robert F. Kennedy was as hard-nosed as they got, one of the inner circle advising his brother, JFK, during the most terrifying moments of the Cuban missile crisis in October 1962, but who also toured the country as a presidential candidate in 1968 asking the idealistic question "Why not?" as he pushed for a radical transformation of American society and a new social compact that would include the traditionally marginalized. "Kennedy's 1968 presidential campaign spoke to themes of grassroots politics and shared governance that the Obama campaign has exemplified," Harry Boyte and University of Pennsylvania historian Steven Hahn wrote in an op-ed published in the Minneapolis *Star Tribune* as the primary season wound down.[3]

From the get-go, Obama has always run as an anti-spin politician. That doesn't mean his campaigns are handler-free or devoid of focus-group sessions. But it does imply that, while the "change" mantra, as a broad transformative promise, is kept deliberately vague, on specific issues he tells it as he sees it to a degree rare among modern politicians. In behind-the-scenes sessions with his handlers, he's quick to tell them that he wants to stay focused on complex policy goals rather than trying to score cheap political points by maneuvering his opponents into awkward votes on the Senate floor or pandering to public opinion when that opinion runs against his own core values.

"He wants to stand politics on its head," journalist Hank De Zutter concluded in his profile of the state senate hopeful published in the *Chicago Reader* in late 1995. "Empowering citizens by bringing together the churches and businesses and banks, scornful grandmothers and angry young. Mostly he's running to fill a political and moral vacuum."[4]

As a community organizer, Obama always told local activists to "take the high road." Two decades later, his friend Loretta Augustine-Herron returned the favor, writing him a letter during the dog days of the presidential campaign reminding him not to abandon that high road in the face of a dizzying array of dirty tricks and smears launched by his opponents; not to sacrifice principle for expediency.

If focus-group findings point out a way to make the communication of a policy point he's already decided on more effective, well and good—but if the focus group tells him his issue is wrong, he won't U-turn to please the pollsters. He uses focus groups frequently, but not primarily to determine policy. Rather, says Stephen Heintz, he and his team employ them "to determine how to communicate his core message in a way that would resonate with the American public."[5] It's a political approach that stands in stark contrast both to Clinton's handlers' preoccupation with focus groups and to the Karl Rove–dominated GOP, a party that passed ostensibly "pro-life" laws to block the euthanasia of Terry Schiavo, a young woman who had been in a vegetative state for years, not because the medical record was flawed but because any and all "pro-life" legislation was guaranteed to act as red meat for the conservative base. As such, the approach serves as something of an antidote to the cynicism so many Americans came to feel toward politics and politicians in the decades preceding Obama's presidency.

MUD WRESTLING DOESN'T DO THE TRICK

One of the most remarkable of Obama's political skills is the fact that he's a quick study, one who soaks up huge amounts of information at great speed, with the ability to absorb the lessons of past mistakes.

When Obama lost the Congressional primary to Bobby Rush in 2000, he learned the importance of coalition building and of not fighting political battles on an opponent's chosen ideological and rhetorical turf. Thrown on the defensive by Rush's allegations that he was something of an interloper, a stranger to Chicago's tough South Side, Obama let the incumbent determine the tempo of the race. It was a mistake he'd not repeat again.

Four years later, he committed a different rookie's error when faced with an opponent's verbal onslaught. Running as the Democratic nominee for an open U.S. Senate position, Obama allowed himself to get visibly riled in his television debates with the ultraconservative Republican candidate, Alan Keyes. Keyes, a fellow African American, accused Obama of tolerating genocide against blacks because of his support for abortion rights. He labeled Obama as un-Christian in his policy positions, and flat-out declared that were Jesus alive in 2004, he could never have voted for Obama. To top it off, he derided Obama's slightly uncomfortable, hedging-his-bets answers on gay marriage. Keyes, a fundamentalist Christian who never allowed his doctrinal beliefs to be challenged by self-doubt, believed homosexuality was an abomination, a sin. Obama believed that sexual orientation was a personal issue; he supported civil unions, but he also felt that marriage should be reserved for the bringing together of men and women. It wasn't Obama's most intellectually coherent position, and it left him slightly vulnerable during the debates.

Keyes's attacks were so personal that, despite their ineffectiveness, they irritated Obama. He forsook his even-keel demeanor, hunched his shoulders during the head-to-head debates, lost his normally laserlike eye lock on the audience, and ended up appearing almost shifty as he tried to look anywhere but at Keyes. "I found him getting under my skin in a way that few people ever have," Obama acknowledged in *The Audacity of Hope*. "When our paths crossed during the campaign, I often had to suppress the rather uncharitable urge to either taunt him or wring his neck."[6] It was a rather tame admission—Jimmy Carter once talked about having the occasional lustful thought, at a time when many fellow politicians were being brought down by actual sex scandals. Obama's admission might be put in this same file, his violent fantasies against Keyes being trivial compared to, say, President Andrew Jackson's long history of actually killing men in duels. But for a man who prided himself on never losing his cool, it was a powerful acknowledgement of how far Keyes had knocked him off his chosen stride.

When it came to his answers, though, Obama more than held his own. And because most Illinoisans viewed Keyes as a fringe firebrand, the Democrat's election came to be something of a given weeks before Election Day. But Obama himself wasn't satisfied. He knew his debate performances had been below par, he knew that a large part of his appeal was his smooth demeanor, and he was determined that next time he not slip into the negative body language he had used against Keyes. He began practicing his debating skills for long hours, sometimes bringing in substitutes who could impersonate his opponents and help him hone his style.

True to form, by the time the 2008 primary season rolled around, he was able to generally battle his opponent to a draw on the issues during the epic series of debates between him and Senator Clinton, while at the same time coming across to viewers as the far more telegenic candidate. And by the time the presidential election sprint itself got going, Obama had become a first-rate debater.

Top-notch lawyer that he was, he was careful to leave no hostages to fortune; and he used his debating skills to neutralize attacks—the attempts to link him to William Ayers, for example—that would likely have sunk, or at least severely maimed, a lesser politician. He parried his opponents' moves, carefully followed their arguments, and then attacked their logical weak spots. His answers were sober and intellectually weighty, and his tone implied not impatience with his antagonists so much as a sorrow that they were not able to reason with quite the alacrity that he could. "Look," he often began an answer by saying, before going on to clearly detail why he supported or opposed a particular policy. It was as if he were telling his opponent to concentrate hard, to make the effort to follow his line of reasoning. Intellectually swift, he could turn an answer about his relationship to Bill Ayers into a larger discourse on the need to get beyond partisan bickering and focus on issues, such as access to health care, that really have an impact on people's lives.

In many ways, he was doing in the debates what he had done during his years in the Senate in D.C. He had buckled down, built up a solid voting record that was safely liberal but not too radical, and largely eschewed rhetorical fireworks. With his eyes on the White House, the lawyer-*cum*-senator had no wish to say and do things that could fracture the coalitions solidifying around his putative candidacy. There was, he intuited, a time and a place for going out on a limb. He had done so repeatedly during his earlier years in public office, and when considering a run for the U.S. Senate he had staked his reputation on a speech in which he opposed the ongoing preparations for a war in Iraq; it was, he declared, a rush into a dumb, unnecessary conflict. Now, with that run for office behind him, he sought to secure his credentials as a statesman, through overseas trips and D.C. alliance building, rather than through sponsoring particular items of high-profile legislation.

On the floor of the Senate and in the hot seat during presidential debates, Obama brought into play many of the skills that he had learned at law school. Chief among these, thought Chris Edley, who had taught the candidate when he was at Harvard and later went on to become dean of the law school at the University of California at Berkeley, was an ability to think as one's adversary would. "There are some things about legal training that I believe are particularly valuable in that line of work. The simplest of those is that we try to drill into our students the importance of thinking about the other side of the argument. A good litigator, for example, knows that in order to prepare your case you have to think about what are the best arguments that the other side has, so you can anticipate those, think about the counterarguments, think three moves ahead. That produces a habit of mind in which you are always testing assertions from multiple angles to see whether they hold up under tough scrutiny. So that's obviously helpful when you're trying to make a difficult political and policy judgment." It was, in many ways, like learning to play chess. The result of such a habit, Edley believed, was a "balanced, dispassionate, analytical approach," one that stood in stark contrast to the "chaotic, mud-wrestling style of policy debate" that too often passed for leadership in modern-day America.[7]

In 2008, during an election season in which disillusionment with politics-as-usual had reached fever pitch, this training helped make Barack Obama a strikingly strong candidate. He wasn't a run-of-the-mill hack, a man who would say anything just to win a few more votes; rather, he was thinking issues through with the voters. He might not be the most exciting debater in the field, but he generally came across as the most thoughtful.

Yet it wasn't just that Obama could think long-term when approaching policy issues. He also had a phenomenal ability to make links between different themes, to understand how application of the law could impact a wide range of societal questions. Instead of compartmentalizing issues, Obama thought holistically. "Really terrific students become adept at fine surgical slicing and dicing of complex problems. Peeling the onion, layer by layer. Whatever metaphor you want to use. But exceptional legal minds can do that but also step back and think about the broader theoretical issues as well as the practical circumstances. And that happens a lot less often than one might imagine, in part because legal training focuses on narrowing and concentrating your analysis rather than being able to step back and think creatively. But Barack, even as a student, had it all," observed Edley. Other

Harvard professors, including Laurence Tribe, who decades later advised presidential candidate Obama on judicial issues, noted the same skill.[8]

In a class that Edley taught on education reform, Obama steered the conversation from one on disparities of educational resources in different communities to legal challenges that could be used to tackle workplace discrimination and unequal employment opportunities. "It was a really sophisticated point," observed the professor, and well beyond the range of most of the other students. For a man not yet thirty years old, this was, Edley felt, extremely mature thinking, and it made the professor all but certain that his protégé was going to go far in life. "I guess over the course of my twenty-eight years as a law professor, there've been a handful of students that I knew I wanted to buy stock in them, because I just had so much confidence that they were going to go on to something great. And Barack was certainly one of those."

In 2008, television viewers tended to agree with Edley's observations. Instant reaction polls after the debates suggested majorities of voters felt Obama had bested John McCain in each of their three head-to-heads. His body language was poised, his answers measured and to the point. When he spoke, he developed an instant rapport with his audiences. Whether in Springfield or during televised debates in the years following, noted Obama's state senate colleague John Milner, a homicide detective who specialized in the analysis of body language, he wouldn't cross his arms or turn away, or do anything else with his body to alienate the people he was engaging with. Instead, "he'd lean toward a person—leaning indicates interest. Barack would be able to talk to that person, find something that person might believe in. Begin to nod his head. The person across from him, who didn't agree with him necessarily, would start nodding his head too. It's a gift."

With the exception of his debates against Keyes, Obama was careful to hold in his anger when his opponents needled him. "He *does* get angry," Milner believed. But he knew how to mask the emotion. "One of the things he does is flash a nice smile when he's starting to get a little angry. It makes him look good, makes him look safe." His smile, said Milner, "is his pause look. He gives himself a chance to regroup a little bit. He's very controlled in his body language. He knows how far he can go; he knows when he has to stop. He learned from the Keyes debate. When he was getting riled up, his handlers told him, 'You can't do that anymore.' Barack's a quick study. He said, 'You're right.' If you look at the Keyes debates up to the debates with John McCain, his body language has changed significantly."[9]

There was, at times, an almost Zen-like calm to the candidate. The effect of this, as John McCain found to his discomfort, was that he became almost impossible to throw off message. He was like 1970s tennis icon Björn Borg, an ice-man playing to win the game—in this case politics and elections—rather than to beat the individual opponent. He kept away from personal attacks; and, when it suited him, generously agreed with his opponent— "I agree with what John said," he affirmed numerous times during the debates—before launching into a discourse about the policies under discussion and why he actually had a different or more expansive approach to the problem at hand than did his opponent.

Doctors' reports indicate that Obama has lower-than-normal blood pressure (90/60) and a slightly slower-than-normal pulse for a man of his age.[10] (Borg, too, was renowned for keeping his heartbeat slow even after hours of strenuous exercise. It was part of the cool-under-pressure mystique that so wowed fans back in the 1970s, during the years in which he won back-to-back French Opens on the slow clay of Paris and Wimbledons on the fast grass of London.) Obama liked the cool aura he projected; it allowed him, he told an interviewer for *Rolling Stone* magazine, to sneak up on opponents in the political arena without them seeing him coming.[11] It made him a peculiarly effective performer under the bright glare of television studio lights. "It's in part his personality, in part his thought process, and the way he then translates his thought process into spoken word," explains Rockefeller Brothers Fund president Stephen Heintz.[12] "The coolness of his persona and the coolness of the media match so well that he just is ideal for it."

PLAYING FOR KEEPS

The myth of how Obama found his way into politics has it being almost by accident, a stumbling in the dark between various careers and musings about possible sources of employment. The reality is more calculated: Harvard law professor Alan Dershowitz believes, with hindsight, that he was eyeing a public career as early as his undergraduate years, when he transferred from Occidental to Columbia. Certainly by the time he arrived in Cambridge to attend Harvard Law School he was already thinking big.

Obama won the presidency of the *Harvard Law Review* by convincing conservatives, in a racially polarized university setting, that he was a liberal they could work with. It wasn't that he was a chameleon—he wouldn't say things he didn't believe in; rather he had the ability to persuade people to work with him, even if they didn't share all his goals and were well aware that he disagreed with their worldview. Said his friend Ken Rolling, a longtime advocate for education reform, "He likes opposing opinions and opposing data, or whatever. But then he wants to work out 'so how do we bring them together and move forward?' He wasn't namby-pamby about it, he wasn't like, 'I'll do whatever you want to do.' He wasn't an appeaser. He's a mediator. He'd demand that we didn't just go off and piss people off."[13]

Later, as a state senator, critics charged that oftentimes he simply voted "present" during votes on controversial issues such as changes to the state's abortion laws. The vote allowed him to say he had participated in major debates, but it also permitted him to avoid taking sides, and thus losing some potential supporters, on emotional wedge issues. The criticism might have been overblown—after all, Obama, a protégé of then–State Senate president Emil Jones Jr., did develop a strong legislative track record in Springfield, sponsoring significant ethics reforms and changes to the criminal justice system, among other achievements—but it hinted at the young politician's useful ability to emerge from melees unscathed.

In all of the political settings Obama has found himself in over the years, he has quickly mastered the rules of the game. He understands how to create close-knit teams of top operatives, how to reach out to audiences and build bases of support. When colleagues during his organizing days told him he should join a church, because he was working with a church-based organizing group, he eventually settled on Trinity United. At least in part, his friend Reverend Alvin Love believed, his choice was likely influenced by geography: Trinity was just a couple blocks outside the catchment area of the Developing Communities Project. Were he to have joined a church inside DCP's zone of influence, a large area of real estate that covered much of South Side Chicago, he would likely have alienated other congregations within the area for slighting them. *We're all involved in fighting the good fight. We all open up our church basements for organizing meetings. So why did he choose that church over mine?* In opting for Trinity, a place of worship intimately connected with the historically African American South Side but not directly involved in the community campaigns embraced by DCP, he sidestepped this hazard.[14]

As he was rising up the political ladder in Illinois, Obama successfully worked out how to forge links with influential figures in a state notorious for its hardball, often corrupt politics yet at the same time to stay above the fray. He navigated the backwaters of a world in which many participants roll around in the mud—witness the legal travails of Illinois's ex-governor Rod Blagojevich, caught by an FBI wiretap talking about selling off President Obama's vacated Senate seat, and in general the culture of pay-to-play politics in the state—but he managed to keep himself clean. The allegations about his relationship with corrupt developer and wheeler-dealer Tony Rezko never really took root. And the hardball tactics his campaign used to keep incumbent senator Alice Palmer off the ballot in 1996 when Obama was running for state senate—his operatives successfully challenging the validity of her nominating petition signatures—were within the letter of the law, even if they somewhat diluted Obama's claims to be promoting a newer, kinder brand of politics.

Over the years, he picked better and more influential teammates. He befriended Emil Jones Jr., a longtime state senator who became Illinois senate president in 2002, when the Democrats finally regained a majority in Springfield. And he then convinced Jones to let him sponsor choice bills and thus curry favor with key party constituencies. In a much commented on incident from the months leading up to Obama's entry into the U.S. Senate race, Obama told the state senate president that he, Emil Jones Jr., had the power to make a U.S. senator; and when the older man naively, or perhaps just disingenuously, asked "who?" Barack calmly replied that he was talking about himself. Obama wanted to head to Washington, and by polishing his Springfield image Jones could help him on the way.

Jones, a onetime Chicago sewer inspector who wanted to leave his mark on the country's political scene but didn't himself have the abilities to go beyond state-level politics, was intrigued by Obama. Perhaps the young man's move to Washington would be his legacy. The president of the Illinois state senate began using his influence to raise Obama's profile; and then, when the U.S. Senate seat opened up, to block Obama's primary opponents from gaining influential endorsements.

At the same time, Obama cultivated many of the city's powerful liberal patrons, men and women who could both raise money for a candidate they liked and also introduce him to ever more senior members of the country's political establishment. By 2004, as he finalized his run for the U.S. Senate, he had come under the wing of Chicago's most influential political consultant, David Axelrod. With Obama as his client, the consultant glimpsed a possible path to glory.

Axelrod could see that Obama brought to the table extraordinary skills of oratory. Listen to Obama speak, and, in his intonations and cadences, you were listening to a poet, a man self-consciously delivering the meter of history to his rapt audiences using not only the idiom of the day but also the rhythms and cadences of great speakers from the past. It was, said Axelrod's partner, John Kupper, an interesting contrast: The man who, in his personal demeanor was low-key and nondemonstrative, No Drama Obama, was a master at pulling his audience's emotional strings when onstage.[15]

It was, to a degree, a gift akin to high-level method acting. Obama in a diner meeting with ordinary-Joe voters or Obama on a stage in front of one hundred thousand people—or even, as on

Inauguration Day, two million people—would be as caught up in the respective moments as, say, Marlon Brando in *A Streetcar Named Desire.* "Define the difference between your behavior and the character's," Stella Adler, method acting's great theoretician, posited. "Find all the justification of the character's actions, and then go on from there to act *from yourself*, without thinking where your personal action ends and the character's begins."[16] Obama would *become* the politician he was expected to be in each given situation, perfectly meshing his persona and his tone to meet the needs of the moment, bringing to bear the full force of his intellect and all of his empathetic abilities to win over his audiences.

On the advice of Axelrod, and with Michelle's help—she had worked in City Hall for several years—as well as that of his close friend Valerie Jarrett, the anti-machine politician feinted toward the power center again. The pragmatist in him started making nice with Mayor Daley's machine; he toned down his criticism of the city's advocacy for splashy developments in poor neighborhoods, and ultimately even let his words be used in promotional material on behalf of the consummate machine mayor. "I don't think there is a city in America that has blossomed so much over the past couple of decades as Chicago. And a lot of that has to do with our mayor. He has a national reputation that is well-deserved," a Daley mailing quoted Obama as saying in early 2007.[17] When he arrived in the U.S. Senate, in January 2005, he managed to get himself some plum committee memberships. In the four years during which he was a senator, he sat on the Foreign Relations; the Environment and Public Works; the Health, Education, Labor and Pensions; the Homeland Security; and the Governmental Affairs committees. He also chaired a subcommittee on European affairs. Methodically, he increased his influence, charted a course toward the locus of power.

ROADS TO POWER

As early as 1992, when Barack Obama and Michelle Robinson tied the knot, at the Trinity United Church of Christ, Obama was already at the center of a powerful, ambitious coterie of liberal, educated Chicagoans. "It was clear to me and to my wife, when we showed up at the church, that we were at the wedding of the year at the South Side of Chicago. That was pretty darn clear," Ken Rolling recalled. Valerie Jarrett was in the pew right behind the Rollings. David Massina, at the time Mayor Daley's chief of staff, was sitting nearby. Jesse Jackson's daughter sang a song as a part of the ceremony at the exclusive South Shore club to which the revelers repaired for dinner. "While he was working very locally, he was being very smart about reaching out and making contacts that first of all began to be citywide, and he was reaching out and figuring out ways to meet people even at higher levels. He was always looking to build wider and wider circles of relationships," recalled Rolling. "He didn't flinch at reaching out and meeting people in a very systematic way. He systematically was widening the circle of people to meet. He was willing, and wanted, to sit down with business leaders; was looking to meet with longtime civil rights, civic, and activist types with long histories in the city;

and people with money and the influence that that bought. It's amazing to me how those circles kept widening out. I think he was very determined to get there."[18]

Of course, the widening circles still left some people feeling excluded. Many politicians in Springfield, particularly other African American legislators from the Chicago area, resented his sense of destiny, the seeming effortlessness with which he glided between worlds. Some pretended they couldn't pronounce his name. Some accused him of being too smart for his own good. There was, during these years, a Gatsby quality to him, a sense that whatever he touched would sparkle. And that quality could spur distrust. For alderman Toni Preckwinkle, Obama's decision to not cede ground to Alice Palmer in 1996, while politically the right one to make, nevertheless said much about the man. "He was willing to take on significant criticism in the service of his own ambitions," she says guardedly. She speaks in code again when asked whether she likes Obama the person. "I have tremendous respect for what he has accomplished," she eventually replies.[19]

And yet, once he became powerful, many of his critics were allowed to enter his charmed circle, were made to feel welcome and significant. Obama is a canny politician who has the skills to render his opponents ineffective and the wisdom to then reach out to them to draw them back into his operation after he has effectively neutered them. Take state senator Rickey Hendon, for example. He was a man who had managed to get No Drama Obama into at least one screaming match while in Springfield, in part by implying that Obama was something of a carpetbagger, that he wasn't "inner-city" authentic. Years after that episode, Hendon wanted nothing more than to be Obama's friend. The superstar politician was, he now declared, "a fine gentleman."[20] *Did he dislike Obama?* Hendon got very angry, very quickly. "I don't care what people write about me anymore, nor do I care what people say about me anymore. And that's just the way it is. I'm tired of trying to deny that I don't like Barack Obama." It was, he averred, "straight bullshit" that he didn't get on with the new president. He had campaigned as hard as anyone to ensure Obama's election to the presidency. Congressman Rush, who had delighted in humbling Obama back in 2000, now declined all interviews on the topic and let it be known through his spokespeople that he had made his peace with Obama and was happy to consider the president a personal friend. Quite possibly these men wanted to be on Obama's good side simply because he was now so powerful. Yet plenty of presidents have carried over feuds with individuals from earlier in their careers. Obama, however, seems to go out of his way to defuse these tensions. It was a part of his notion that differences could oftentimes be set aside simply through good, old-fashioned communication.

While Obama received solid marks from liberal groups for his voting record in the U.S. Senate—despite his caution in sponsoring bills that could be labeled in some way "radical," the *National Journal* went so far as to rank him the most liberal senator in 2007[21]—he wasn't averse to ditching pledges popular with liberals and alienating left-leaning constituents when it seemed pragmatic to do so. Witness his promise, early in the presidential campaign, to restrict his fund-raising in order to run a race paid for by public funds—long a clarion call for progressives interested in reforming the electoral system. Once it became clear that his candidacy could out-fund-raise any and all opponents, however, the pledge was quietly put to one side and private funds, to the tune of many hundreds of millions of dollars, began pouring in to the Obama campaign.

Nearly a year after that volte-face, Obama perturbed some liberals again, by going out of his way to woo conservative opinion makers: in the run-up to his swearing the oath of office, he convened a much-publicized meeting with right-wing bloggers and newspaper columnists—giving them more time than he had given bloggers on the progressive end of the political spectrum. On the eve of his inauguration, he hosted a dinner for his vanquished opponent, John McCain. And on the day of his inauguration, he had evangelical pastor Rick Warren, who had alienated progressives with his perceived homophobic rhetoric in advance of California's vote on the anti-gay-marriage Proposition 8, give the invocation prayer. It was both a nod to Warren, who had invited the presidential candidates to his church for an early-season town hall meeting, and, more generally, a signal of conciliation to an evangelical community still reeling from its loss of influence in the November elections.

Disarm your opponents through grace. John Kennedy was a master at the art. When the renowned scientist Linus Pauling, who had won the Nobel Prize for chemistry in 1954, criticized his administration for its resumption of nuclear weapons testing, Kennedy responded by inviting Pauling and other Nobel laureates to a black-tie dinner at the White House, during which he and Jackie Kennedy assiduously courted their critic. When students convened on Pennsylvania Avenue to protest the confrontational nuclear policies of the U.S. and Soviet governments in February 1962, the president ordered his kitchen staff to provide the shivering demonstrators with cups of hot coffee and cocoa. Give succor to your opponents, even while not ceding significant policy ground to them. Let a conservative, Rick Warren, give the invocation, but then feint left again by having a civil rights veteran, the octogenarian Reverend Joseph Lowery, read aloud the words of the African American "national anthem," "Lift Every Voice and Sing," during the inauguration's closing benediction.

There is, Obama clearly believes, no sin in temporarily disappointing, or even bemusing, his key constituents if, in so doing, he can clear pathways for his main legislative agenda and the realization of his core ideals.

A MASTER OF THE GAME

Despite that ever-widening circle that Rolling had identified, in many ways Obama is still a surprisingly solitary figure—a person who has always had to fight to create a niche for himself, who has always been visibly different from most of those surrounding him. That self-containment is a core part of his identity. Watch

Barack Obama in action, and you are watching a political Grand-master (the president is a chess player, though he references the game only rarely) or a highly talented poker player; someone who has learned to play out complex strategic games in his head, who has learned to heed, and to synthesize, the counsel of others and ultimately to harness his own inner strength when making decisions of import. Watching Obama dismantle opponents over the weeks and months of his campaigns, you are observing someone unfathomably skilled at the ruthless game of politics who has, simultaneously, perfected the fine art of elegant, mannered, intellectual fencing. He's a tiger with the disarming smile of a Cheshire cat. He calls for an end to "politics as usual," and yet he is one of the greatest practitioners of the craft.

In the boxing ring, Muhammad Ali would tease his heavier, stronger opponents, wearing them down with the feathery, dance-like qualities of his movements until he was ready to nail them against the ropes. Obama, on the political stage, exudes a similar effortlessness. That doesn't mean he never makes mistakes— witness his calling working-class voters "bitter" midway through the primary contests—but it does imply that, when he does, he's nimble enough to speedily contain the damage. He has the instincts to know what needs to be done to make things right in a hurry when he errs.

In describing Obama the politician, friends and colleagues use two words that don't necessarily sit together easily. Time and again, one hears that Obama is both a pragmatist and an idealist. He is driven by ideals, but he doesn't want to sacrifice power simply to maintain a romanticized sense of purity. He does what he has to do to stay on top of the game. In a May 2009 interview with *New York Times* reporter David Leonhardt, Obama declared his own economic policy compass to be guided by a "ruthless pragmatism."[22] And yet, he also clearly has ambitions to not just tinker with individual problems but to fundamentally remold the American economic and political model.

So which comes first, idealism or pragmatism? "Ooooh, that's a good question," Reverend Alvin Love responds, drawing the words out slowly as he shapes his response. "I *think* he's an idealist first, and then perhaps his idealism may get structured by his pragmatism." He emphasizes "think" to make it clear he's not entirely decided on the issue. "He may actually envision that anything can happen. Great possibilities. Now, how does that get done? The pragmatism comes in and shapes that idealism. You have to be an idealist first, as an African American, to run for president. You have to believe that kind of thing can happen. The pragmatism then gives it a framework. Pragmatism would have said, 'Look, an African American can't be elected president.' So, I'd say he's an idealist first. He envisions what *can* and what *should* happen."[23]

CASE STUDY

THE IOWA CAUCUS

As a candidate for high office, Obama has clearly always believed that he rides the waves of history. Without this historical gut-check, it is impossible to understand the logic that propelled him from a charismatic, but overwhelmingly junior, figure at the 2004 Democratic Party convention to a man throwing his hat into the presidential ring less than three years later.

What made a black man with almost no national experience believe he could win the Iowa caucus? What made him think that a majority of caucus voters in one of the whitest states in the country would listen to his words rather than simply look at his skin color? What made him so sure that those early opinion polls showing Hillary Clinton with a twenty- or even a thirty-point lead among likely caucus voters were wrong? By no conventional political calculus did Obama's decision to aggressively contest Iowa make sense; yet in hindsight, we can see that Obama—like the

Catholic John Kennedy, believing he could win over Protestant primary voters in 1960—had read the moment perfectly.

For Reverend Alvin Love, at least part of this assurance came from Obama's work with organizers in one church basement after another in South Side Chicago during the mid-1980s. Working in those settings, Love believed, was somewhat akin to the intimate, hands-on work involved in building trust and support among caucus voters in a state like Iowa. It wasn't all about the sound bite and the media blitz; instead it was about getting to know people, listening to their stories and telling your own. He kept coming off as "likable," remembered *Des Moines Register* political columnist David Yepsen.[1] "That smile. His kids were an asset. His wife turned into a real asset. She was out here doing events on her own, and getting great crowds. There was a warmth there, a personal connection that he had with people who were out here." Media consultant Axelrod and campaign chief David Plouffe were, said Yepsen, "able to bottle and can that enthusiasm. It was just very methodical. I'll give you an example: You'd have these huge crowds that would show up [to Obama rallies]. To get into the event, you had to go through a little chute—'Are you registered? Do you know where your caucus is?'—People were clearly identified early as Obama supporters. Axelrod and Plouffe are two guys who've done this state a number of times, they understand the culture, and saw to it that he had a superior organization."

At meeting after meeting, Obama would not just speak, but

listen, fielding questions, unfiltered, from his audiences, engaging them on their own level. When a seven-year-old boy stood up during a meeting in the small town of Maquoketa in mid-September 2007 and urged an immediate end to the Iraq War, Obama answered him courteously, combining a sense of seriousness with a touch of humor. The candidate smiled, the *Des Moines Register* reported, and then, before launching into a defense of his plans for a phased withdrawal from Iraq, compared his interrogator to the child TV character Opie, in *The Andy Griffith Show.* The boy was duly impressed by Obama but told journalists afterward that he still supported Clinton. Many others in Maquoketa and elsewhere weren't so sure anymore. The more they became familiar with the freshman senator from Illinois, the more they came to like him. For increasing numbers of Iowans, Obama was both the most credible antiwar candidate and the man who best understood their everyday lives and immediate concerns.

As he barnstormed the state, Obama's ability to engage with audiences attracted more and more supporters to his cause. He was, felt Jason Clayworth, a political reporter for the *Register*, pacing himself perfectly; he hadn't used up all his energy out of the starting gate, hadn't worried about the early polls.[2] Instead, he'd hovered behind Clinton and Edwards, ready for an end-of-year dash to the finish line. By the night of the fabled Jefferson-Jackson dinner, on November 10, 2007, Obama had cemented in place both a cadre of local supporters and a more general image of himself as an apostle of change, an underdog determined to upend the notion of politics as usual.

That evening, he gave a trademark Obama oration, uplift-
ing in its message, soaring in its imagery, scathing in its critique
of a political culture reduced to sound bites and focus groups.
"This party—the party of Jefferson and Jackson; of Roosevelt and
Kennedy—has always made the biggest difference in the lives of
the American people when we led, not by polls, but by principle,"
he told his audience. "Not by calculation, but by conviction; when
we summoned the entire nation to a common purpose—a higher
purpose. And I run for the Presidency of the United States of
America because that's the party America needs us to be right
now. A party that offers not just a difference in policies, but a difference in leadership. A party that doesn't just focus on how to
win but why we should." He talked of closing Guantanamo Bay
and restoring habeas corpus. He spoke of tackling nuclear pro-
liferation and seriously addressing climate change, of providing
health care to all and raising the minimum wage. He envisioned,
he said in conclusion, nothing less than "a nation healed. A world
repaired. An America that believes again."

Obama had laid the gauntlet down. The junior senator from
Illinois was now the man to beat. By the new year, with just days
left until the caucus, polling conducted by the *Des Moines Register*
suggested that he had taken the lead among likely caucus voters.

A few months earlier, when Obama was talking about construct-
ing a plane as it was taxiing down the runway, the Senator had
gambled that he could put together a team of operatives who would
be able to sell him to the overwhelmingly white caucus voters in

Iowa. Were he to fail, his candidacy would likely be stillborn. In succeeding, however, he would begin the long process of convincing skeptics that he was both qualified enough to be president and also able to connect with enough white voters to neutralize the impact of racial prejudice during a grueling presidential election campaign. That would win him the support not just of more white primary and caucus voters in states whose elections followed fast on the heels of Iowa's, but also of African Americans—who, initially, supported Clinton over Obama, largely on the assumption that the Illinoisan couldn't win.

By the time the caucus neared, Obama's campaign had thirty-seven field offices dotted across Iowa. The operation dwarfed those put together by Hillary Clinton and John Edwards. At the Boomer Café, next to Obama's Des Moines HQ, Sasha and Malia Obama could sometimes be seen eating chocolate chip cookies. Soon, the owner was selling "Obama cookies" by the thousands, each one a de facto sugary advertisement for the candidate.

Already raising huge amounts of money, Obama began using his Hopefund political action committee to dole out campaign contributions to an array of state politicians running for election or reelection. In return, they offered him their endorsements. The intent, from day one, was to put cracks in Hillary Clinton's veneer of invulnerability, to weaken her simply by making her appear a political mortal.

Undermining Senator Clinton in little ways as well as big ones was important, for the assumption that she was unbeatable, that her candidacy was a fait accompli, was the chief reason many people were supporting her in the first place. Sure, the Clintons had many die-hard fans who would vote for Hillary either on her merits or out of loyalty to her husband no matter what. But others simply wanted to glom onto a perceived winner. She was the juggernaut candidate. If Obama was going to spoil her party, he had to do so from the get-go, before she acquired an unstoppable momentum. Should he lose Iowa, primary season would essentially be over before it began; if he won, it would be a long winter and spring.

As at so many other key moments in his meteoric rise, Obama got lucky. Or rather, when his opponents fouled up, he knew how to seize the moment. Clinton's team was decidedly sloppy going into Iowa. By contrast, many of Obama's inner circle were masters at milking the complex caucus system to their candidate's advantage. "Plouffe had worked in the Iowa caucuses for Dick Gephardt [in 2004]. We had actually done the Iowa caucus for Paul Simon when he ran for president back in 1988," explained Axelrod's partner John Kupper.[3] "We'd done it four years earlier for John Edwards. There were a lot of people associated with the Obama campaign who had prior experience in Iowa. I don't think there was a similar experience on the other side, because frankly Bill Clinton never really competed in Iowa."

In 1992, then-Governor Clinton, immersed in an early season sex scandal, had virtually ceded Iowa to home-state native Tom Harkin, banking instead on a strong finish in New Hampshire to make his reputation as the "comeback kid." Sixteen years later, his wife's campaign, overly reliant on lessons learned during Bill's long-shot journey to the White House, made the fatal mistake of underestimating the psychological significance of a loss in the country's first caucus to an insurgent campaign such as Obama's. Hillary's problem was that, in many ways, Barack Obama's candidacy was more akin to Bill Clinton's than was hers. Obama was the young, charismatic underdog taking on the party establishment. Clinton, by contrast, was now the ultimate insider.

As Obama built up his support with literally dozens of visits to the state—during many of which he made a point of stressing his anti–Iraq War credentials to likely caucusgoers of a liberal bent, touting his "judgment" as being a better guide than his meager executive "experience" as to what kind of a president he would be—some of Clinton's advisers even urged her to pull out of the caucus to concentrate on bigger prizes down the road. The front-runner was off to an appalling start, ceding ground not just to Obama but also to ex-Senator John Edwards.

"Our folks had a very deep understanding of how the caucus process worked and how you could use the caucus process to maximize your advantage and maximize your delegates," Kupper explained. They knew, for example, that in rural precincts you needed fewer votes to secure a delegate than you did in the large cities; thus, while Clinton mainly campaigned in urban hubs like Des Moines and Waterloo, Obama hit rural spots, many of them in solid Republican territory, looking to pick up a delegate here, another there. He ran television ads featuring Kirk Dillard, a Republican colleague from his days as a state senator, singing his praises and touting his ability to work across the aisle; that was important, recalled John Kupper, since focus groups AKPD Media had conducted showed that even the most partisan of Democratic caucus voters responded well to candidates who could put aside petty party squabbles to work on sorting out big-picture problems such as poor access to health insurance and the war in Iraq.[4] His team put hundreds of volunteers through "Camp Obamas," training them to go out into communities and tell the candidate's story, go out and talk to people about their hopes and fears. They were, observed Marshall Ganz, using the power of narrative to familiarize voters with Obama and make them feel like they had a personal stake in his success.[5]

For reporter Yepsen, the Obama campaign was a revelation. "I've covered these caucus campaigns going back to Jimmy Carter. Generally you win a caucus fight by finding people, getting them out and you just get more people than your opponents. It's pretty straightforward. What Obama did in some precincts, he saw he had not just enough votes to win, but enough to make sure Clinton finished third. It was important at that stage of the race for all these other candidates to stop Clinton. Had she won Iowa, she probably would have run the table. It would have been like John Kerry in 2004. You win Iowa, you go the distance."

On caucus night, Obama's tech-savvy operators monitored each precinct, regularly communicating among caucus locales with their BlackBerrys. As the voting blocks coalesced, if the Illinois senator had already secured a numeric majority in a given precinct, getting the candidate his needed delegates, the campaign would release some of its surplus supporters to John Edwards, who was running a strong, populist-leaning race in Iowa, so as to knock Clinton down one more notch. "That," noted Yepsen, "was as sophisticated a move as I had seen in a caucus ever. Not only to find enough votes to win, but to dictate the placement of your opponents down below you."

On the day of the caucus vote, Obama played pick-up basketball with a group of close friends. At the time, it was a way to break the tension. Afterward, with Obama winning the caucus with 37.6 percent of the vote, and his decision to release supporters to Edwards nudging Clinton into third place,[6] it came to be seen as totemic, a bringer of good fortune. From then on, important election days were always marked by a game of ball.

That night, addressing a crowd of elated supporters, many of them crying with happiness, at the convention complex in Des Moines, Obama seemed to be floating on a great cushion of confidence. "This was the moment when the improbable beat what Washington always said was inevitable. This was the moment when we tore down barriers that have divided us for too long—when we rallied people of all parties and ages to a common cause; when we finally gave Americans who'd never participated in politics a reason to stand up and to do so. This was the moment when we finally beat back the politics of fear, and doubt, and cynicism; the politics where we tear each other down instead of lifting this country up. This was the moment."

And then, as he did so many times during the campaign,

Obama cornered the market on optimism. "Years from now, you'll look back and you'll say that this was the moment—this was the place—where America remembered what it means to hope."

Say something enough times, with enough fervor, and your words become the received wisdom. If there was any doubt before the January 3 caucus, afterward there was none: Obama was the Democratic candidate best positioned to exploit the country's yearning not just for a change in leadership but for a change in the broader political culture.

CHAPTER NINE

THE INSPIRER

In 1990, Obama wrote an essay for a collection titled *After Alin-sky*. In it, he warned communities not to look for their salvation in great leader-figures. "A viable organization can only be achieved," wrote the twenty-nine-year-old law school student, "if a broadly based indigenous leadership—and not one or two charismatic leaders—can knit together the diverse interests of their local institutions."[1] Yet while he didn't fully admit to it in those early days, even then Obama must have known his own peculiar powers to sway audiences. Too many people had listened to him speak and told him he was destined for greatness for him not to have been aware of this.

For Bettylu Saltzman, a fund-raiser and longtime stalwart of Democratic Party politics in Chicago, her first encounter with Obama left her as enthusiastic as a bobby-soxer at a Sinatra concert. It was 1992 and Saltzman was working for Bill Clinton's team in Chicago; Obama came to talk to them about his voter registration efforts with Project Vote. He oozed confidence and charm, was clearly extremely smart, and, at the same time, could listen to people like no one else she had ever met. She knew, from that moment on, that he would be president.[2] She told her husband this. More important for Obama, she also told her friend David Axelrod. *Call Obama,* she urged him, during one of their regular early morning calls, at which they shot the breeze about basketball and politics. *This man will be president one day.* Axelrod told her she was surely exaggerating, but he agreed to put in a phone call. It didn't take long for him to become as impressed as Saltzman.

Later on, Saltzman and Obama would run into each other at their neighborhood Whole Foods store; they also attended many of the same political gatherings and parties. Saltzman started inviting him to any and every soiree she could think of at which she could introduce him to politically influential Chicagoans. The Obamas sat at Saltzman's table at an Alzheimer's charity gala honoring her, and at a New Israel Fund event. She became, for Obama, something of a patroness, introducing him to the powerful Ladies Who Lunch club—a group of nineteen affluent liberal women in Chicago, including Hugh Hefner's daughter Christie, who have played a key role in shaping more than a few political careers in the Windy City—and to other scions of Chicago's political and financial establishment. "I always felt that if there was ever an opportunity to have him be someplace where he could meet more people, then I would try to do that," she recalled. "I saw his political abilities. I thought that he was one of the . . . I guess I thought he was one of the smartest politicians I had ever seen, also one of the most intelligent human beings—all those things we all saw in the campaign; I saw the germ of that. His ability to draw people in, his ability to talk to people one on one, look people in the eye and talk to them." There was something about the young man, something almost impossible to put a finger on. He just had a *presence*, a sense of stature surrounding him. When people came up to Saltzman and the young man accompanying her, she would introduce her companion as "our future president." *How did he react to this?* "He didn't back off. He didn't say, 'Oh, no.' He smiled."

When the Evanston Democratic Party held a slating session in late 2003 at which all the party's U.S. Senate hopefuls laid out their cases and sought the chapter's endorsement, Obama began the evening as simply part of a crowd of talented, well-connected politicians. Because party rules mandated that the chapter couldn't endorse one candidate unless an overwhelming 80 percent of the attendees came out in favor of that person, it was a pretty good bet the night would end in stalemate. Instead, Obama spoke for a few minutes, and, according to his golfing buddy Whitman Soule, "just absolutely knocked everybody over."[3] "He ended up polling over ninety percent of the people who were there, and got the endorsement. There was just this 'wow' factor." By the time his law firm colleague Bill Micili opened his house up to host an Obama fund-raiser a short while later, the word had gotten out: This was a different kind of politician. Micili's house ended up full to bursting with people there to see a man they thought could one day be president.

MATINEE IDOL ON A MISSION

Obama knows that he has a peculiarly empowering effect on people, and, like John Kennedy in the early 1960s, he harnesses this energy to bolster his political position, using every medium available to spread his message and connect with his audiences.

Kennedy used television to ruthless effect during his presidential debates with Richard Nixon. Those who heard the debates on the radio tended to judge Nixon the winner. Those who watched the two duke it out on TV, who saw Nixon, with his notorious five o'clock shadow, sweating under the hot lights, his body language awkward, his face a bundle of nerves, and who saw Kennedy next to him, his perfect teeth flashed in perfect smiles, his body at ease, overwhelmingly judged the Massachusetts senator to be the victor. Unfortunately for the Republican, television was the hip new medium, and JFK's presence dominated viewers' screens.

So, in 2008, Obama's campaign made sure his supporters saw him not just on television but on the Internet. His image was all over YouTube. Obama speeches went viral within minutes of being made. His supporters banded together into Facebook communities. Even his pick of vice-presidential running mate was built up into a high-tech drama. Give the campaign your cell phone number, aides announced, and you would be text-messaged with the announcement as soon as it was made public. Huge numbers gave up their cell phone contact details, which went into vast campaign databases used subsequently to rustle up donations, phone bank volunteers, and canvassers.

Partly this was a techno-gimmick designed simply to expand the Obama campaign's pool of potential foot soldiers. Partly, however, it was a conscious effort to make these foot soldiers feel empowered and so get them to act innovatively in spreading the candidate's message of change. "Of crucial importance for the possibilities that long term change might grow from the campaign, civic agency found expression in the field operation," wrote Harry Boyte afterward, in a report for the Kettering Foundation.[4] "The field operation incorporated advanced technologies, from FaceBook to text messaging." But, Boyte continued, the most important secret ingredient was empowerment. "Everyone has a story, everyone is unique, and everyone has dynamic potential as a creative agent."

Within the sometimes byzantine world of community organizing, individuals and groups split into many different categories. There are Alinsky-style organizers, who often put a premium on confrontation. There are mobilizers, people who prefer to lead a small cadre of disciplined apostles of change rather than to build broad movements. And so on. Organizers can be, and generally are, members of more than one category. The borders, often fluid, between the categories tend to be hard for outsiders to glimpse. And yet, to those who spend their lives doing this work, they are important. One category is known as broad-based organizing. It combines grassroots work with an appetite for intellectual ideas and solutions. This more cerebral, scholarly approach is one that many of Obama's mentors back in the 1980s adhered to. It is, say people such as John McKnight, the rightful heir to Democratic Populism. This was the set of ideals that fueled the farmers' movement of the eighteenth and nineteenth centuries, the workers' movements of the 1930s, and King's civil rights movement. When King talked of a beloved community, he envisioned a body of people linked together not just by material interests but, as important, by values and ideas.

The famous civil rights advocate Ella Baker, a superb practitioner of broad-based organizing, wrote that part of the job of a good organizer was to keep people's worst impulses in check and encourage them to express their best impulses. Obama is strikingly good at formulating this notion: At a 2006 Book Expo America event, while sitting on a panel alongside the novelist John Updike, he told a Washington, D.C., audience that "we all have a stake in each other; my success is directly tied to the success of my neighbor . . . we're tied up in a mutual destiny. And every so often this expresses itself in our government, in our collective life, and it's that sense that propelled me into politics."[5] *Work together, put grievances to one side, harness our collective energies, and the sky's the limit.*

One day, when he was on a Senate trip to Israel, Obama's Harvard buddy Hill Harper phoned him reminding him about a literary promise he had made. Obama had agreed to write a short piece for Harper's book, a motivational tract for young black men, but now, despite the fact that Obama and a few other contributors hadn't yet come through, Harper's publishers were demanding he submit the manuscript the very next morning. Harper explained his dilemma, and Obama stayed up late into the night writing the passage, which he then e-mailed to Harper. "Life is what you make it," the senator wrote. "Those who achieve don't waste time on self-pity. They don't spend time focused on how unfair life is. They don't blame other people for their problems and they don't use race or poverty or hardship as an excuse for failure."[6]

Obama sets high standards—he talks of "the project of American renewal"[7]—and en masse, people seem to want to live up to his expectations of them. It isn't simply that he's a smooth operator; almost by definition any successful politician is somewhat smooth. Bill Clinton, for example, was a master at making people feel he understood them, got them; "I *feel* your pain," will likely remain one of his most enduring lines. But at least in part there was a neediness behind this: Clinton desperately wanted to be liked. It was, in many ways, an overriding concern for him. Part of what sets Obama apart is the fact that, over and above the sense of efficiency and competence, he inspires audiences not just to like him but to *trust* him. Part of his appeal is that audiences want to feel for him, to get him, almost as much as he feels for them. People listen to Obama and they *want* to believe. They look out for him not just as a politician but almost as a member of their family, a talented son sent out into the wider world to bring honor on his community. His glory reflects back on them.

In that way, Obama is similar to Muhammad Ali. True, Ali was vainglorious in a way Obama isn't, but both share a rare ability to transfix an audience. "Suddenly I realize the obvious," wrote author Davis Miller in his 1996 book, *The Tao of Muhammad Ali*.[8] "That I've been acting like a teenage admirer again. And that Muhammad Ali has not lost perhaps his highest talent—the ability to transport people past thoughts and words to a world of play. Being around Ali, or watching him perform on TV, has always made me feel genuinely childlike. Today, I'm not troubled at all by my own problems. I look at his family: They're beaming. Ali still flips their switches, too."

"I cared for him the way I cared for my children," Loretta Augustine-Herron, one of Obama's closest friends from his organizing days in the mid-1980s, remembered in wonder. "I felt protective of him. I just really wanted to make sure that he was alright. I knew he was away from his family. He was always such a good person, caring, really did care about people. I understood how hard he worked, and that a lot of that work was done for us. And we weren't paying him very much. He started off on ten thousand dollars, with a three-thousand-dollar bonus to buy a car. He worked every day; he worked hard every day; he worked long hours every day. That's a once in a lifetime thing, that somebody comes into your life and actually cares about how it turns out. I felt very protective, very motherly toward him. I was so glad when he got married. He had a wife. He was going to be happy." For Herron, her encounters with Obama had been transformative. "Sometimes," she wondered, "I don't know if he really understood how appreciative I was for the things that he taught me. But I was. It was one of those things that really increased the quality of my life, and allowed me to help others go as far as they could go and understand they were of value. It's amazing what one person can do for you, if you're willing to learn and listen. He had such a gentle way of talking with you and keeping you kinda focused on what as a group we needed to do. He had such a gentle way of nudging you right in the direction he wanted you to go."[9] Her best friend, Yvonne Lloyd, who recalled her great-grandmother telling her stories from her childhood as a slave, agreed. She watched Republican Party figures mock Obama for being "only" a community organizer, and her mouth fell open in amazement. "They don't realize what impact that made on the lives of those people in that area. It may not seem like anything to anybody else," she explained, "but he did a lot to raise us up. And then after he left, with the training we had gotten from him, we kept going. We kept being involved, and kept doing things. It helped our community very much. Yes, he's something else. He's the one that I'm glad that came along in my life when he did—because it made a lot of difference."[10]

Now, with her friend president of the United States of America, Loretta Herron wanted to ask him one question: "How does it *feel*?" She felt a tremendous sense of pride, a sense of communal ownership of his stunning achievement. "Basically I know he'll do a good job. I know he'll be a people's president. Someone asked me, did I think he owed African Americans something. And I don't think so. Any debt that he would have owed us was totally wiped out when he attained the Oval Office. Once he became president, it took away the myth about how far we could go and who we could be. We can be anybody we want to be. He did that for us. That's something you can't put a price tag on. Now his job is to be the president of all people and restore America to her proper place in the world, with the respect of people. And I think he'll do it."

PROPERTY OF THE WORLD

Throughout the presidential campaign, Obama volunteers were taught to tell stories, both their own and that of their candidate. Marshall Ganz's Camp Obama sent thousands of young men and women onto the streets of cities and hamlets across the country, putting out a message carefully tailored to trigger feelings of hope and of empowerment. They were taught to explain how to build community, they were taught to listen as ordinary people told them their hopes and fears.

On Martin Luther King Day, the day before he was inaugurated president, Barack Obama returned to his community organizing roots. He donned jeans and a work shirt and, with cameras in tow, headed off to a shelter for troubled teenagers in a poor, run-down neighborhood of Washington, D.C. There the man who within hours would be the world's most powerful person rolled up his shirtsleeves and set to work, painting the walls of the homeless shelter. All around the country that morning, in response to Obama's pleas for a national day of service, volunteers were turning up at local charities to donate their time and energies.

"Here is the life principle of democratic planning," Saul Alinsky wrote in *Reveille for Radicals*.[11] "An awakening in the whole people of a sense of this common moral purpose. Not one goal, but a direction."

They responded to Obama's call not because they were coerced but because they felt empowered. The country's new leadership was something to take pride in.

Opinion polls from early in Obama's presidency showed a public both deeply enamored of their new leader—a *New York Times* poll from inauguration week put his favorability rating at well over 60 percent[12]—and also willing to grant him years to turn the poor economy around. While solid majorities during the last years of the Bush administration felt the country was heading in the wrong direction, equally solid majorities in early 2009 believed Obama had the capacity to get the country back on its feet again.

Of course, great expectations can generate great disillusionment. New York University sociologist Troy Duster thinks the comparison between Obama's election and that of Nelson Mandela, in South Africa, is apt. When Mandela attained power, in 1994, after nearly a half-century of apartheid rule, a sense of euphoria swept his country. *Anything was possible*, was the sense on the ground. The reality, however, was messier. Apartheid had created deeply ingrained inequalities: Whites had attended better schools, had accumulated more capital, had more experience running businesses and so on. After the euphoria ebbed, the inequities remained. And within a few years, a potent current of disillusionment ran through much of South African life, expressed through soaring violent crime rates and renewed cynicism about the powers of government to do good. "Hope, aspiration, desire is one thing. But that comes at a price. Illusionment and disillusionment are related," explains Duster.[13] In Obama's case, however, the stakes are even higher, because the expectations are global.

Americans expected miracles from Obama; after watching one country after another undergo its own velvet or satin revolution in the years since the Berlin Wall fell in 1989, America could now plausibly claim to have undergone its own cathartic changing of the guard. But it wasn't only his fellow countrymen who had great hopes for Obama. So, too, did the hundreds of thousands of Germans who had thronged to Berlin's Tiergarten to hear him speak in July 2008; so, too, did the huge crowds who attended him when he visited Kenya and South Africa on a congressional delegation in 2006. So did the millions around the globe who thronged to election parties to celebrate the Illinois senator's victory. Obama had become, quite simply, the property of the world. And in doing so, warned Duster, in some ways, the capacity for disillusion had become far greater.

How Obama navigates the minefields of economic devastation and foreign resentment bequeathed him by his predecessor will determine whether he remains an inspiring figure throughout his presidency. Charisma, says Duster, involves two things: The first is force of personality, which Obama clearly has in abundance. The second is a relationship with one's audience. Put another way, it takes two to tango; a politician can be as suave and articulate as can be, but if those listening and watching are unwilling to be seduced, his message will fall flat. "If the audience doesn't respond," explains Duster, "the charisma isn't there."

In his first months in office, however, Obama seemed largely to be retaining his appeal. His popularity ratings were high and, while the public was nervous about the state of the economy, his broader agenda for change enjoyed wide support. "Everybody is able to see a little piece of themselves in Barack," David Axelrod's partner, John Kupper, believed, "and his aspirations and his accomplishments."

CASE STUDY

TEAM OF RIVALS REDUX

On December 1, 2008, Barack Obama strode onto the podium in Chicago. Behind him were heavy blue drapes and a phalanx of American flags. The president-elect wore the colors of the stars and stripes: a dark blue suit, a white shirt, a red-striped tie. To his left was vice president–elect Joe Biden. To his right was his longtime primary season nemesis, Hillary Rodham Clinton.

Senator Clinton was, Obama told the assembled press corps, his choice for Secretary of State.

It was a bold move. America's fifth-youngest president was surrounding himself with erstwhile political foes who could plausibly claim to have far more hands-on policy experience than did he. Biden had been an early contender for the Democratic Party's presidential nomination—a role he had coveted since he first ran in 1988. The Delaware senator had been on the Senate Foreign Relations Committee for years and prided himself on his expertise on international affairs and national security issues. During the primary season, he had lambasted Obama, albeit to almost no effect, for his lack of foreign policy experience. Obama's first choice for commerce secretary was New Mexico governor Bill Richardson, another presidential hopeful who had come into primary season with the advantage of an extraordinary résumé— over the years he had been a governor, a U.S. congressman, energy secretary, and special envoy to North Korea—but had failed to engage with caucus and primary voters. He was talking with Iowa governor Tom Vilsack about his becoming secretary of agriculture. It was quite a change in fortune for Vilsack, a man who had taken on something of an attack-dog role on behalf of Hillary Clinton during primary season (people who worked with Vilsack recalled that Hillary had once told him that he reminded her of her husband, only without the flaws). The president-elect wanted Robert Gates to stay on as secretary of defense, despite the fact that, under President Bush, he had presided over the ongoing war in Iraq, a military adventure that Obama staunchly opposed.

Now Barack Obama was executing his bravest personnel decision; he was hiring Clinton—whose campaign had run the notorious "three A.M. phone call" ads, challenging Obama's competence to respond to emergency situations, questioning whether he had the mettle to be president—as the nation's premier diplomat.

It clearly wasn't done out of affection for the Clintons—they had, after all, been thorns in his side from the Iowa caucus right through the convention, with Bill dismissively terming his ascendancy a "fairy tale" during the hard-fought primaries and Hillary negotiating for a place in the convention spotlight at Denver that overshadowed Obama himself during the first couple days of the proceedings. But while he might not have liked the ex-president and his wife on a personal level, he clearly respected the New York senator's political power and her intellect. He didn't necessarily want her as his vice president—not least because her husband would have been part of the package, bringing a commander-in-chief's ego and strong political instincts directly into the White House inner sanctum—but he did want her on board in a major role as his administration got under way.

The appointment demonstrated both a remarkable self-confidence—elevating a woman who clearly at one time distrusted and disliked him, who viewed him as a parvenu, to one of the most senior positions in government—and also an understanding that it is often better to silence critics and their support base by co-opting them rather than leaving them to snipe from the sidelines.

By now the comparisons with Lincoln's Team of Rivals have been made so often they have practically entered the common lore. That said, they are worth reiterating. After winning the 1860 election, Lincoln—a relative neophyte who had edged out three far more senior Republican Party figures in securing his party's nomination—brought his rivals into a virtual national-unity administration as the country fissured around Southern secession. William Seward became secretary of state; Salmon Chase was appointed secretary of the treasury; and Edward Bates was made attorney general. Not content with reaching out to foes within his own party, Lincoln also included ex-Democrats, opposed to the South's course of action, within his cabinet.

Lincoln's success in holding such a potentially fractious administration together, wrote the historian Doris Kearns Goodwin in *Team of Rivals*, "suggests that in the hands of a truly great politician the qualities we generally associate with decency and morality—kindness, sensitivity, compassion, honesty, and empathy—can also be impressive political resources."[1] Through four years of civil war, as the Union teetered on the brink of an abyss, Lincoln would remain, in Goodwin's words, "master of the most unusual cabinet in the history of the country."[2]

In late 2008 and early 2009, President Obama was trying to pull off a similar trick, bringing together an A team to pull the country out of deep domestic and international crises. Its members didn't all share the same political perspective; they certainly didn't all see eye to eye with the president on every issue. But as did Lincoln before him, Obama believed the members of his administration would work together effectively to bring the country through its trials. There was, Goodwin told Nebraska Public Radio on the bicentenary of Lincoln's birth, "nothing wrong with having him as a mentor" when standing on the world stage.[3]

Like Lincoln, and also Franklin Roosevelt, Obama favored divvying up assignments so that more than one senior administration official would be working through the same significant policy problems at any moment in time. In Lincoln's case, he would encourage open competition over policy; FDR was more subtle or, to put it less delicately, devious, oftentimes not telling cabinet members that he had assigned the same problem to two different individuals or teams.

Obama began building up dual-tier systems for making decisions. In addition to his cabinet secretaries, he appointed a number of policy "czars" charged with coordinating a range of policy responses—from how to deal with climate change and create green jobs through to how to tackle poverty, urban and housing policies, and the country's growing health insurance crisis. (At the same time, he resisted the urge to appoint a car czar to deal with the near-bankrupt automakers, ultimately relying on a small group of senior advisers to navigate Chrysler and GM's slide toward insolvency. And he also turned down entertainer Quincy Jones's pleas to create a "culture czar" position.)

In addition to the domestic policy czars, he appointed special envoys to Afghanistan and Pakistan, and to the Middle East, envoys who would operate almost as mini-secretaries of state for their designated regions.

The czars represented something of a personal brain trust, people accountable directly to the president, without large bureaucracies and Cabinet offices behind them. They wouldn't supersede cabinet members, but they would operate on something of a parallel track to them. Not everyone was enamored of the strategy. Obama's use of these czars, opined West Virginia Senator Robert Byrd, the nonagenarian who had carved out a venerable reputation over the decades as a defender of Congressional oversight prerogatives, was too great an extension of White House powers. But, supporters countered, the use of czars allowed for a more unfiltered policy debate, creating positions held by people answerable only to the president—a man who showed every sign of wanting vigorous policy discussion among his advisers rather than a chorus of tired policy recommendations from people beholden to bureaucracies that in turn were beholden to a Congress still much in thrall to special interests. It was, they argued, a logical extension of the practice Obama had developed as a senator of going outside the reservation: of calling on writers and scholars whose work interested him to discuss their ideas and of asking Congressional Research Office personnel to hold tutorials and seminars for him on issues he wanted to get up to speed on. He wasn't looking for uniformity of opinion; rather he wanted competing views. As such, the reliance on czars was, in many ways, a throwback to the improvisational policy-making process Franklin Roosevelt utilized when developing the institutions that formed the bedrock of his New Deal.

These habits, in turn, were learned from his days as a community organizer and voter registration coordinator. "Barack had to both directly manage a staff of organizers and bring together a broad spectrum of community organizations, many of which had been at odds with each other; bring them into that effort and manage to do it in a way which remains the most successful nonpartisan voting project in Illinois history," Project Vote's funder Sanford Newman recollected.[4] "He was rigorous. He believed in accountability and results. Extraordinary maturity in dealing with problems. And extraordinary judgment. He was surprisingly mature. Negotiating a potentially treacherous, fractious, intra-organizational political situation to get everybody pulling together for the same cause. It took a lot of judgment about how to handle people." In a roomful of men and women, Obama would make sure to get everyone's opinion. He was, in some ways, still the university lecturer, still trying to get the silent kids in class to venture out of their shells. It was, said John Kupper, a trait "quite unusual" in a politician of Obama's preeminence. Such figures were, the media consultant had found, "used to having the stage and hearing themselves talk."[5]

President Kennedy's aide Richard Donohue compared Obama's brain trust to his onetime boss's fabled Camelot administration—except, he believed, Obama's team was more talented, and Obama perhaps a better foil to their strong egos. JFK had a sharp tongue, which he wasn't afraid to use to cut down or intimidate people he disagreed with. Obama, by contrast, didn't use humor to demean his opponents. JFK, a child of privilege, could be extremely catty toward men he loathed, such as General Curtis LeMay, dismissing them from his presence and then cruelly bad-mouthing them before those colleagues who remained. Obama always took care to show respect even to those he disagreed with. He might go after their ideas aggressively, but he would never go after them as individuals.[6]

From the get-go, Obama has made it clear that he doesn't like yes men, that he prefers advisers who force him to think more carefully through his positions. This is, in part, an innate Obama characteristic. It is also something honed by his experiences at the

University of Chicago, an academic culture renowned for undiplomatic intellectual confrontations and a no-holds-barred debating climate. While outsiders oftentimes find the university's culture somewhat obnoxious, its proponents are adamant that it's not about being ornery for the sake of being ornery; rather it's about forcing people whose ideas put them in the spotlight to carefully evaluate, and then reevaluate, their positions. It's a way to keep intellectually fresh, to not sit back and rest on one's laurels. "It doesn't matter who you are, you walk in the room, you have to justify your existence every time. At the University of Chicago, the proper response to even the most withering question is not resentment but gratitude," explains Obama's erstwhile colleague Geoff Stone. "This is a tough, demanding, no-bullshit place. For Barack to be steeped in that place, as he was not only by teaching courses in law school but by being a really visible and central resident of the community, I have no doubt it's had a dramatic impact on his way of thinking, his way of building a cabinet, the lack of angst about disagreement. The willingness, indeed the eagerness, to bring in people who will disagree with one another and disagree with him."

The University of Chicago, and the surrounding Hyde Park community, averred Stone, created "a capacity to generate disagreement, to understand and promote disagreement without it becoming uncivil," and a strong sense that the best ideas came not out of kowtowing to one's colleagues but out of "intellectual conflict."[7]

Others saw something of the Harvard Law School in Obama's

emerging executive style. Good litigators, said Chris Edley, detailing Obama's law school–honed skills, learn how to work with experts from many different fields, as they compile depositions and more generally build their cases. It cultivates a habit, Edley argued, "of really thinking like a general contractor. Recognizing that you are going have to pull from lots of different sources in order to develop the best line of argument or the best analysis of the problem, rather than thinking you know it all."[8]

Obama's team of rivals and, more generally, his layered system of advisers and policy czars, was, in many respects, another version of the elite lawyer's crew of experts. It was a way of maximizing the input of ideas, of forcing open policy doors too often kept barred in Washington, D.C.

CHAPTER TEN

THE LEADER

Throughout his career, being in the presence of power has not intimidated Obama. As a young organizer, he would meet with city officials with no sense that there was an imbalance between him and the people he was speaking with. As a law student, he would talk as an equal with Harvard deans. As a fresh-out-of-school lawyer, he would engage in spirited conversations with heads of multibillion-dollar foundations. Obama has never wimped out in challenging environments. And yet he isn't bullheaded. He listens at least as much as he talks, and on those rare occasions when he has tried too hard to show his smarts—in early meetings with other Joyce Foundation board members, for example—he has correctly read the unease of his colleagues and modified his behavior accordingly. During what can only be seen as a meteoric career, he's not been infected with what state senator Bill Haine termed "the House of Lords attitude,"[1] the sense of entitlement that so many politicians seem to acquire as their careers advance. In fact, says one of his close friends and advisers, while some people acquire an "imperial" attitude along the road to supreme power, Obama had "gotten more humble as the years have gone on." He had, the friend felt, become "more down to earth, more comfortable with people, a better listener."

If effective leadership in an open democracy like the United States is in large part about communication, Obama has the perfect leadership personality. He has the confidence to insert himself into any situation and, at the same time, to listen and learn from others. He knows how to frame his ideas in a way that brings people on board rather than scares them away, thus maximizing the size of the coalitions that he can build around issues he cares about. "It's definitely a leadership skill and a capacity to do two things at once," said one longtime Obama observer from Chicago's foundation world. "To allow people of a like mind and interested in addressing these issues to feel there really is a chance to change things. And, secondly, making people who are uncomfortable with the change occurring more comfortable." He would, the observer commented, get people to "taste change."

In the early days of his presidential campaign, when the betting classes still had Hillary Clinton down as unstoppable, Obama flew out to Los Angeles. Eric Garcetti, the L.A. city council president and Obama's campaign chairman for southern California, had convened a meeting with Latino- and immigrants-rights advocates at an atmospheric old Mexican restaurant on the city's famed Olvera Street. The Illinois senator faced a wall of skepticism: the Clintons were highly regarded among Latino voters, and

Obama was seen as something of an unknown quantity. After an hour of discussions around the tables of the dimly lit La Golondrina café—during which Obama ate nothing—he had managed to convince them that, in Garcetti's words, "he was the real deal."[2] Later, Obama walked down the cobbled streets of Old Town and over to Union Station with Maria-Elena Durazo, executive secretary of the Los Angeles County Federation of Labor, talking with her one-on-one. Soon afterward, Durazo announced her support for Obama and took a leave of absence from her job to campaign for him.

"His strengths are at the subconscious level," Garcetti decided, after watching the candidate in action. "It's not what's said on the surface. I think people get a feel for who he is. He doesn't come in and kind of say, 'Let me lay out for you how closely I've worked with Latinos in the past.' He just lays out who he is, in a very relaxed and straightforward manner." For Garcetti—a Democratic Party convention superdelegate who had been wooed heavily by Hillary Clinton's campaign in the weeks before he threw his support to her opponent—while Obama's oratorical skills were impressive, even more important were his listening skills, his ability to convince people that he cared about their opinions.

Those skills had served him well throughout his career. Back in the late 1990s, when state senator Obama proposed legislation that would track police officers' racial profiling of minorities during traffic stops, he worked hard to get conservative colleagues aboard the issue. When he proposed reforming state licensing requirements that excluded ex-felons from an array of jobs—

including those, such as barber, for which they had received training while inside prisons—he did the same thing: long meetings with opponents, phone conversations with concerned attorneys from regulatory agencies. He smoothed out the kinks in his legislation, making it as easy as possible for law-and-order legislators to support it. To the surprise of criminal justice reformers in Illinois, the legislation passed. Said one such reform advocate, Obama took on "issues that were really toxic on some level and figured out how to design a bill and move on it."

Bill Haine, who sat on the state senate judiciary committee with Obama, recalls that the Hyde Park liberal achieved a similar consensus around his campaign to reform the state's death penalty and police interrogation requirements, successfully pushing through legislation mandating that interrogations of suspects be videotaped. Haine, a conservative older Democrat who had served as state's attorney for Madison County for fourteen years, was deeply impressed by the way in which Obama reached out to prosecutors like him and his Republican colleague Ed Petka for advice. "He doesn't burn bridges. He's back frequently to seek input. He sees the process as an end result rather than his just getting 'my way.' He was a remarkable legislator. He always sought to develop as much as possible a bill which would accommodate most if not all of the objections of those who had problems with the bill. You can't satisfy everybody. But he would go a long way toward crafting a bill where the opponents might not be for the bill, but they'd be neutral, which is important. The very effective senators are affable, bright, and willing to talk. They don't ever become truculent or personal about opposition. They're willing to see all sides, but they're not going to give up their core position, so there's a personal integrity there."[3]

Obama, said media consultant John Kupper, had an "instinct" for reaching out to any hand stretched across the fence by an opponent. If he had a shtick, it was that in an era in which too many ideologues were hell-bent on ripping apart the social fabric, he was a healer, someone who knew how to repair the frayed canvas of modern-day America. He had core values, but he wouldn't browbeat his opponents when they disagreed with him. In the U.S. Senate, he would work with dyed-in-the-wool conservatives, such as Oklahoma senator Tom Colburn, on issues they could agree on—legislation to put the federal budget online, for example, so that taxpayers could easily see how their money was being spent—and he'd oppose them on issues over which they had fundamental policy differences. In both situations, however, he'd make a point of staying civil.

When President Bush convened an emergency White House meeting at the height of the financial meltdown, bringing together McCain, Obama, and other senior political figures, participants recall that Obama repeatedly asked his GOP opponent: "Where do you stand, John?" On one level, they saw it as Obama laying down a challenge, forcing McCain to take positions on controversial bailout measures. At the same time, Obama, the younger, less experienced, but more intellectually agile candidate, was going out of his way to seek unity during a time of grave economic danger. Later on, as a newly inaugurated president pushing a near-trillion-dollar stimulus package in the face of Republican congressional opposition, Obama made a point of talking with Mark Zandi, a senior McCain adviser on economics. Zandi was one of the few Republican economics spokesmen to make sympathetic noises about some parts of the huge stimulus bill, and Obama realized the publicity value of having him on board. Working across the aisle, Kupper argued, was "good politics. It's what Americans want. What voters want. They want to see their leaders try to work together. Even if you only get two or three votes [from the opposition party] on the stimulus package, at least you've made the effort. Maybe it paves the way for more cooperation down the road."

WHEN HALF THE HOG IS AS GOOD AS IT GETS

That belief in the virtues of collaboration, in the need to create a broad tent for one's proposals, dated back to Obama's days as a South Side Chicago organizer. And the belief that he was the man best suited to raising that tent, that he was born to perform on the political stage, went back almost as far.

When Obama returned to Chicago, in 1991, with a Harvard law degree in hand, he met with his old colleagues at the Developing Communities Project. John Owens, who had taken charge of the organization three years earlier, remembers that Obama made it clear that he no longer wanted to be seen as a community organizer. He was, he told Owens, ready to be a leader; he wanted to give speeches and put his own name and face in the spotlight. It wasn't a statement uttered in arrogance, Owens felt, merely a matter-of-fact notice of intent.[4] Obama had come to realize he shone when that spotlight homed in on him—in truth, he'd always had an inkling of this, at least since the day when he picked up a bullhorn and addressed a group of antiapartheid protestors at Occidental College in the early 1980s, luxuriating in the enthusiastic crowd response his words generated—and he wanted to craft for himself a career in politics.

Saul Alinsky, the guru of Chicago organizers, would have understood: in his most famous book, *Rules for Radicals*, Alinsky wrote that rather than whine about antiwar protestors being brutalized by American soldiers and police officers, young people should "learn a lesson. Go home, organize, build power and at the next convention you will be the delegates."[5] Organizing and politics weren't cast in perpetual opposition; rather, they were two sides of the same coin.

In 1993 three large foundations—MacArthur, Joyce, and Spencer—were approached by local education reformers Ann Hallett and Bill Ayers, of aforementioned Weather Underground notoriety. A few months earlier, the philanthropist Walter Annenberg had laid down a challenge to America's largest cities: Come up with viable plans to improve failing schools, and he would seed these programs to the tune of fifty million dollars . . . *if* the city reformers themselves could come up with one hundred million. Hallett and Ayers had put together a proposal and, to their astonishment, had received word from Annenberg's office that the fifty million was theirs for the taking. Now all they had to do was come up with their own one hundred million dollars. The two education reformers had no idea how to raise this kind of cash, so they punted the challenge over to the three foundation heads.

Barack Obama's name was mentioned as a possible chair for the Annenberg Challenge Board the foundations needed to set up. He was, said someone from the Joyce Foundation, a talented new civil rights attorney in town. Patricia Graham, a Harvard education professor who was, at the time, also in charge of the Spencer Foundation, recalled that she had read about Obama during his *Harvard Law Review* days, and she decided to call him, invite him out to dinner, and sound him out about the Challenge.[6] They met for a late supper at Avanzare's Italian restaurant, on Superior Street, and, after talking until the tired restaurant staff was practically sweeping the floor around their feet, Graham offered the young attorney the job. As a strikingly talented black man raised by a single mother, he could become, she felt, "a powerful symbol for minority kids in poor schools in Chicago."

Once on the board, Obama more than lived up to Graham's expectations. He would speak to teenagers in dilapidated inner-city schools and hold them spellbound. As important, he had a knack for hiring talented board members, and in a city renowned for you-scratch-my-back-I'll-scratch-yours politics, he was determined to hire only men and women of integrity, people who would spend the $150 million dollars at their disposal on programs that worked rather than just ones touted, for various pork-barrel reasons, by individual politicians. He would grill researchers on the information they brought to him, fruits of large-scale longitudinal studies on education reform, and he would insist that they fully explain the implications of their often arcane findings to him and his board-member colleagues.

And yet, while he understood the need to master detail, overall he was not a micromanager. He was, says Ken Rolling, who also served on the Challenge's board, far more intrigued by the big picture. He preferred coming to an understanding of an issue and then delegating responsibility for implementing the details to competent staffers. He was also, Rolling came to see, impatient with abstract ideology, preferring pragmatic approaches that could be shown to bear results over one-size-fits-all education theory.

The same results-based approach held, whatever policy conundrum Obama approached and at all stages of his political career. Sit down with Obama, felt John Trasviña, president of the Mexican American Legal Defense and Education Fund (MALDEF), and you were sitting down with a person stripped bare of all intellectual pretenses. He would, literally, roll his sleeves up and get to work. When the pair met in Obama's somewhat sparse Senate offices in 2006 to talk about immigration reform, the Los Angeles–based MALDEF executive felt he wasn't talking to a politician but "to someone who says, 'OK, cut out the pretense. What's on your mind? And what are we going to be doing together?' His years as a community organizer in Chicago are really very, very close to him."[7] Obama seemed to come at issues from a personal basis; immigrants weren't, for him, an abstraction, and the perils of illegally crossing a border and then living without legal papers in the shadows weren't mere talking points in a policy debate.

The junior senator had angered some Latino immigrants-rights activists by voting for the Secure Fence Act of 2006, legislation that channeled money into a large border fence project. He had justified his vote, part of an 80–19 majority, by asserting that he didn't want to marginalize himself in future policy discussions around immigration by straying too far from the center on this issue. Coming down in favor of the fence would, he argued, allow him to propose less punitive immigration reforms down the road; would allow him to support devoting resources to improving the economies of Mexico and Central American countries, so that fewer people felt compelled to journey north and illegally enter the United States in the first place. Obama asked MALDEF and other activist groups to give him some room on the issue—after all, he and Ted Kennedy were the only two senators who had joined immigrants-rights marchers during the huge May Day protests earlier that year. *Surely*, he seemed to suggest, *that gave him some credibility.*

The senator was doing what he did so well, blending idealism and pragmatism. He was voting for a largely symbolic fence because it was the pragmatic thing to do; he was protesting the harsh treatment of immigrants because it was the idealistic response to a situation in which millions of people were being scapegoated for a country's ills. A few months later, after Mexican

American citizens in Orange County received flyers in the mail erroneously informing them that they could be arrested and deported if they attempted to vote in upcoming elections, Obama sponsored legislation intended to get the U.S. Justice Department more actively involved in stopping local voter intimidation. The measure didn't pass, but the anger articulated by many activists around his Secure Fence Act vote largely dissipated. Two years later, Democrats in Congress prepared to send similar anti-intimidation legislation to President Obama for his signature.

Obama's onetime Harvard tutor, Chris Edley, felt the president was demonstrating a combination of a lawyer's pragmatism and an organizer's idealism. Good lawyers, and by extension effective leaders, Edley believed, knew their opinions weren't the only ones worth hearing, they knew that at the end of the day most decisions involved a degree of give-and-take. "It's hard to find a good lawyer in public life who is self-righteous. Because being self-righteous is incompatible with a good lawyer's analytical turn of mind. You're prepared to go to a table and negotiate, to recognize you don't have the one truth," said Edley. Of course, there was a potential downside to this: "If you don't have a moral compass, then it's all about the deal, it's all about getting to yes. I used to accuse the Clinton administration of a 'let's make a deal' approach to the presidency. So that's something to watch out for. The fact that you're willing to negotiate doesn't mean that everything should be negotiable. You have to have the skills of a lawyer, but you also have to have values that define your leadership." His protégé's moral compass, Edley intuited, was in good working order.

Onetime state senator Denny Jacobs, Obama's poker pal in Springfield, believed him to be a "resilient realist," a man who could be knocked down but would quickly get up, dust himself off, and start all over again. "He knows what he wants, and he has tremendous ideals of where he wants to go. But I also think that he's realistic enough to understand he probably is not going to get all of it."[8] Witness the $787 billion stimulus package he got Congress to pass three weeks into his presidency. It contained more tax cuts than he had originally wanted and slightly less money for public works projects. But it was, nevertheless, a startlingly ambitious package. "If you know what your convictions are, then you're in a position to compromise," Obama averred shortly after he was elected to the U.S. Senate. "When you don't know what your convictions are, then it [politics] becomes a sport."[9] Obama knew when to fight the good fight and when to back down and compromise. He knew, as all great leaders do, when to accept what Jacobs memorably termed "half the hog."

"WHY WASTE A GOOD CRISIS?"

By 2009, thirteen years after first winning a state senate seat in Illinois, Obama had ascended the mountain and sat atop its peak. He remained a charismatic loner, a man with the ability to sway tens of millions with his words, and the hunger to make his mark on history.

America's forty-fourth president assumed office with the economy in free fall and America's international reputation in tatters. Within minutes of his being sworn in and giving his inauguration speech, in front of an estimated two million people thronging the Washington Mall—others on the podium with Obama that day recall that the waves of sound reverberating back from the crowd were like nothing they had ever heard before— President Obama was already signing cabinet nomination papers and a proclamation declaring a national day of renewal and reconciliation. Shortly after lunch he was back at work, instructing military prosecutors to temporarily halt legal proceedings involving Guantánamo Bay detainees and issuing orders to government agencies to put a hold on last-minute regulations signed by outgoing president Bush. Perhaps he was recalling words he had uttered twenty-seven months earlier, at an event in Boston's Kennedy Library and Museum. If you run for the presidency, he told the audience, you make a bargain with voters: trust me with ultimate power, and in exchange I will be prepared to give my life to the job, to put aside all fear, doubt and insecurity, to acknowledge there will be no time "for sleep, family life, vacations, leisure."[10]

During the days and weeks ahead, the pace didn't slow down. After just over a month in office, he had signed into law the most ambitious fiscal stimulus package since the 1930s—a legislative triumph in pursuit of which the new president had barnstormed the country for nearly a week, urging passage—as well as a huge package of aid to home owners at risk of going into foreclosure. His budget envisaged spending hundreds of billions of dollars on moving the country toward health care for all. He had ordered the gradual shutdown of the Guantánamo prison, in Cuba, reapplied the Geneva Conventions to the treatment of terrorism suspects, and ordered a review of the legal status of the men held without trial during the war on terror. He had revamped America's approach to tackling global warming and had charted a new course regarding discussions with Russia on reducing the two countries' nuclear weapons arsenals. He had ordered a phased withdrawal of U.S. troops from Iraq and an increased number of troops to be deployed to Afghanistan. Obama had also signed orders creating a White House office of urban affairs, opening government decision making to greater public scrutiny and overturning time limits on a woman's ability to sue her employer for workplace pay discrimination.

All told, it was a stunning turn away from the policies and priorities of the Bush administration. And it demonstrated an agenda of extraordinarily ambitious, all-encompassing scope. The huge ship of state was being wrestled onto a new course, was being deliberately turned away from thirty years of neoconservative economics and social policy. As the stock market fell, as unemployment, homelessness, and hunger rose, so the role of government in stepping in to ameliorate the hardship caused by failing markets became more crucial; and far from being intimidated by this prospect, President Obama gave every appearance of relishing the opportunity to transform America. After all, as his adviser Rahm Emanuel was often heard saying, "Why waste a good crisis?"

Ted Sorensen, who had closely observed every administration since that of John Kennedy, was impressed. He believed that Obama had all the qualities of a great president. "A good leader," Kennedy's most faithful adviser opined, "has a lot of followers. He has to have the qualities that attract and hold and motivate those followers. It's not just the speeches; but he's got to get people to tune in and listen to the speeches. Then when they listen to them, they've got to agree with them. Then when they agree with them, they've got to act on them. That's what a leader does. That's what Kennedy did and that's what Obama, I think, will do."[11]

For Sorensen, the young president exhibited many of the same traits as did JFK. He was "calm, cool, and articulate." He had strong powers of judgment. He was comfortable in his own skin. And he was endowed with the twinned qualities of patience and wisdom. Such qualities had allowed Kennedy to navigate the potentially apocalyptic pathways of the Cuban missile crisis. Such qualities ought, he thought, to allow Obama to steer the ship of state through the many security and economic crises confronting early twenty-first-century America. He would, said Sorensen, an old man with a lifetime of political experience, be able to "ride through those storms and prevail."

Obama had spent decades fine-tuning his analytical and communications skills. He had honed his innate political instincts until he outshone all contemporary political figures. And he had mastered the difficult art of truly listening to what his audiences— be they ordinary voters at campaign rallies or powerful colleagues in Washington, D.C.—were saying to him. He had taken huge risks and had been rewarded spectacularly by the country's voters. Now, a new United States of America was being born. And that new America, in its conversations and its priorities, in its sense of self and sense of possibility, would bear the stamp of Barack Hussein Obama.

CONCLUSION

A NEW MORNING

In the early years of the twentieth century, my great-grandparents arrived at New York's Ellis Island, after a weeks-long journey to a land far removed from the pogroms of czarist Russia. They would have stood on the decks of their boats and watched as the Statue of Liberty hove into view. Had they been able to read English, they would have seen Emma Lazarus's words engraved on a plaque inside the base of Lady Liberty: "Give me your tired, your poor, / Your huddled masses yearning to breathe free, / The wretched refuse of your teeming shore." They would have stood up a little straighter and, in Yiddish, uttered words of wonder at the mighty New World awaiting them. When they became citizens, they voted—first the men, then, when women were enfranchised, my great-grandmothers too—that simple act of participating in who governed them marking them out as residents in a land of limitless possibility.

For my forefathers, and the tens of millions like them who

have come to the United States in the decades since, America was so much more than simply a country. It was a breathtakingly audacious concept. The American Dream was, for these migrants, a metaphysical presence, a journey of wonder, a space for reinventing and reimagining human possibilities. In the United States, the myth went, it didn't matter what conditions characterized your birth; what mattered more was what you made out of your life. If there were limits to your horizons, they were self-imposed rather than mandated by the wider culture.

Over the long months of the presidential election campaign, that sense of America being a place where one could at least preserve the illusion that birth wasn't destiny came under intense attack. Bereft of fresh ideas, the Republican Party unleashed a barrage of smears to maintain its hold on power. Obama, senior party figures insinuated, was a terrorist, a Muslim, a socialist, a communist, a radical, an atheist, an elitist.

At the GOP Convention in Minneapolis, ex–New York City mayor Rudy Giuliani could hardly contain his contempt. In Obama, he said, sneering, "You have a résumé from a gifted man with an Ivy League education. He worked as a community organizer. What?" The crowd, on cue, burst into laughter. "He worked—I said—I said, OK, OK, maybe this is the first problem on the résumé. He worked as a community organizer." Sarah Palin accused the Democrat of "palling around with terrorists." He was, also, they kept implicitly reminding Southern voters, in particular, black. They never exactly came out and said it—and by all accounts Senator McCain himself was deeply uncomfortable with any hints of prejudice from within his campaign; but they did keep calling him "un-American," kept asking America "who *is* Obama?" One Southern politician even called Barack and Michelle Obama "uppity"—and then rather implausibly denied that that phrase had a racial connotation.[1]

As the economy tanked throughout September and October and millions lost their investments and their jobs, the attacks grew uglier. Fight the election on the issues, Republican strategists knew, and they would lose. But remind audiences often enough about the color of Obama's skin, the religious affiliations of his father's ancestors, and they thought they could maintain their hold on power. At Palin rallies, in particular, the tone was dark; "kill him, kill him," chants could be heard at some of the more raucous events, as could a steady patter of racial slurs.

Had the Republican Party gotten a majority vote that way, had they managed to retain power despite having brought the economy to the brink of collapse and the country's global reputation to a nadir, the American Dream as a concept would have taken an extraordinary pummeling.

In the weeks preceding the election, that fear was everywhere. Anyone with a sense of history, both in the United States and abroad, could feel it. The GOP strategy, said General Colin Powell, when he endorsed Barack Obama two weeks before the election, was "demagoguery." "This goes too far," the onetime chairman of the Joint Chiefs and secretary of state told news anchor Tom Brokaw. Powell went on to say that he had "heard senior members of my own party drop the suggestion, that '[Obama's] a Muslim and he might be associated [with] terrorists.' That is not the way we should be doing it in America."[2]

On November 4, 2008, in decisively rejecting the timbre of the Republicans' campaign, America's electorate chose to take the country on a dramatically new course. Obama's election to the presidency was, quite simply, a transformative event. From a period of deep national cynicism and despair, the country had journeyed into a moment of almost utopian hope and in so doing had learned to reconnect with its public institutions and broader sense of community.

The possibilities unleashed by Obama's election were redolent of a stanza from a Langston Hughes poem written seventy years earlier. "O, let America be America again," the poet wrote, before he went on to delineate the possibilities of a land, and a dream, remade from the sweat and blood, the hopes and aspirations of ordinary people from all walks of life and all ethnic backgrounds.[3]

Like all utopian moments, there was a risk that this one would not meet expectations, especially given the catastrophic state of the economy and the perilous state of America's relations with much of the rest of the world that Obama's administration would inherit. But that those expectations now existed was a momentous change in and of itself. After forty-plus years of political cynicism and collapsing voter participation—a crisis of democratic faith unleashed by the wave of assassinations of the 1960s, the sordid scandals of the Nixon presidency, and a growing sense that politicians could be, and were, all bought for a price by powerful lobby groups—suddenly America was at a place in which citizens were desperate to once more be able to put their faith in good government and good leaders.

Despite the cynicism of the electorate, Obama had managed to reawaken hope. On Election Day, tens of millions of Americans cast aside their fears, decided to put their trust once more in the ballot box, and came out to vote in record numbers for a candidate they believed would change the country for the better. That huge turnout was, in and of itself, a pivot point for the country; a resurrection of America's faith in its democratic institutions.

Barack Obama's ascent to power signaled a change of historic import. In part, that was because of who he was: The color of his skin alone, as well as the name that he bore, served as a demarcation line between past and future. In larger part, however, it was because of what he represented.

In an era of sound-bite politics, Obama managed to reintroduce nuance into America's political discourse. He reinjected the art of patience, of long-term thinking, into a political culture that had increasingly lurched toward instant-gratification policy approaches. In an age characterized by ever shriller, ever more polarized politics, Obama found a way to bridge divides and generate a renewed sense of community and common purpose. In a moment of rampant cynicism—turbocharged by the Bush administration's misleading statements regarding weapons of mass destruction in Iraq, as well as by the incompetent response to Hurricane Katrina's destruction of New Orleans—Obama reignited Americans' sense of idealism and hope.

Overwhelmingly, voters *trusted* Obama. They believed that he would be honest with them and that he would govern with their best interests at heart; that he wouldn't simply hear their words and then twist them for short-term advantage, but that he would listen to them carefully and genuinely bring their concerns with him if he won the election and moved into the White House. It was that sense of trust that allowed Obama to defeat far more experienced opponents during the grueling Democratic Party primary season; *measure me by my judgment, not my experience*, Obama urged the electorate. And it was that connection with ordinary voters that ultimately propelled him to victory in the presidential election.

For all of these reasons and more, Obama is a once-in-a-generation political leader. He brings to the White House a temperament and an intellect each of themselves rare among senior politicians, but in combination almost unprecedented. And he has ascended to power at a moment both riddled with extraordinary danger and also rife with peculiar opportunity for a country's transformation. If he succeeds, both in stopping the rot and in reinvigorating America's soaring sense of possibility, he will go down in history as one of the country's most significant, most energizing presidents.

"We are the greatest, the largest economy. The most formidable military," ex–New York governor Mario Cuomo averred a week before Obama was inaugurated president.[4] "There are people all over the world, literally, who are praying for the success of Obama, his efforts as president. Because the world economy is affected by the United States; because peace in the world is impacted by the United States. And so Obama's impact on the globe, whether he succeeds or fails, the result of that will affect the entire globe." One of the country's most astute political observers, Cuomo argued that it was a far larger responsibility even than that faced by Lincoln as the country sped toward civil war. "Lincoln's failure would have scarred the United States," said the ex-governor. "Obama's failure can cripple, significantly, the world. Especially on the economic side. Globalization has tied us all together. The world is holding its breath, waiting for Obama. He has the chance to go down as great. What makes people great is crises."

In researching this book, I have discovered no single "Rosebud" person, event, or thing that fully explains the question I set out to answer at the start of this volume: *What makes Barack Obama tick?* What I have found is that he is a powerfully driven man, ambitious, intelligent, and charming. He is a person with many interests and many professional skills. He is an individual with a polyglot background and a set of experiences that predispose him to understand the complexities of life and to recognize the fragility of what today is and the dangers and possibilities regarding what tomorrow might be.

But at the end of the day, none of these traits in and of itself is enough to explain fully either Obama's belief in himself and his abilities to harness the energies of a people and transform a nation or the country's reciprocal faith in him as a leader. Obama the president is a product of a particular moment, a unique confluence of events that cumulatively showed the existing political order to be akin to the fabled emperor with no clothes.

Had America not been bedeviled by seemingly endless crises during the early years of the twenty-first century—from the terrorist attacks of September 11, 2001, through the wars in Iraq and Afghanistan, from Hurricane Katrina through the bursting of the housing bubble in 2007 and the more general economic collapse in 2008—Obama might well never have emerged as a viable contender for the presidency. Instead his boundless energies, his enthusiasm, and his communicative skills would likely have been channeled into other projects. In an era of vast angst, however, Obama became the perfect foil for a national unease, a messenger of hope during years in which many felt despair.

As he navigated the long road to power, Barack Obama fashioned himself as being something and someone new, both a healer and a listener. In telling his own extraordinary life story, he became a repository for all the millions of pent-up stories, all the dreams and vaguely articulated expectations, of his vast audiences. In the years since he had shot to stardom in the wake of his July 2004 speech before the Democratic Party's convention, he had emerged as a one-man embodiment of a revivified American Dream.

Ultimately, even before he had sworn the oath of office, Barack Obama, the man elected to serve as America's forty-fourth president, the man who had once cautioned against putting too much faith in charismatic leaders, had become something larger than an individual. He had become, in short, a living legend.

ACKNOWLEDGMENTS

Writing a book about a figure as enigmatic as President Barack Obama is every political writer's fantasy. For making that fantasy a reality, I owe my agent Victoria Skurnick, and her colleague James Levine, at the Levine Greenberg Literary Agency, thanks beyond measure. Thank you, Victoria, for having faith sufficient in my work to recommend me to Portfolio's editors for this fascinating writerly adventure. And thank you to my editors, Jeffrey Krames and Jillian Gray, for heeding their advice.

Inside Obama's Brain is a book conceived in the last days of autumn, halfway between Obama's election victory and his inauguration. And it is a book written in the first months of his presidency. To the hundreds of people who took time out from extraordinarily busy, chaotic schedules during these transition months to talk with me, either on the record or on background, I owe a debt of gratitude I can likely never repay. From the halls of power in Washington, D.C., to the backstreets of Chicago, the men and women I talked to for this book helped me develop an understanding of the mind-set and motivations of the world's most powerful man. While space does not permit me to thank you all by name, let me use these acknowledgment pages to tip my hat to you collectively.

A few people, however, I must thank individually. To Charlie Halpern, a truly wise man, whom I have known for many years: thank you for your extraordinary insights and for your willingness to meet with me not just to be interviewed but to provide me with detailed editorial observations as the book matured over the months. To Yvonne Lloyd and Loretta Augustine-Herron, who dusted off quarter-century-old memories of Barack Obama to augment my understanding of what the young organizer's presence meant to local residents of South Side Chicago in the mid-1980s. And to Jerry Kellman, Marshall Ganz, John Mc-Knight, Harry Boyte, and Mary Gonzalez for providing me a crash course in the nuances of community organizing both in Chicago and nationally. Your words, and the books you recommended that I read, allowed me to better comprehend the world and the set of philosophical ideals that helped mold Barack Obama. To John Kupper, who served as a sounding board for my developing observations about Obama the politician, I extend my deepest appreciation. Thanks, too, to Miles Rapoport and David Callahan, at Demos, and to Stephen Heintz, at the Rockefeller Brothers Fund. You went beyond the call of duty in reaching out to contacts in the world of politics who could aid me in this project.

It would have been impossible to take a book from genesis to completion within the time limits bounding this project had I not been able to fall back on an all-star roster of friends and family members willing to double as copy editors and critics. As chapters were completed, so the e-mails started flying through cyberspace. To Eyal Press, a dear friend and journalist whom I much admire, thank you for your invaluable comments on how to frame this book. Thanks, too, to Steve Magagnini, who, despite a full writing load at the *Sacramento Bee*, took the time to line-edit several chapters. Your journalism continues to be an inspiration. To my parents, Lenore and Jack Abramsky, and to my wife, Julie Sze, my deepest thanks for similarly, albeit temporarily, making the shift into editorial mode. To Chris Stamos, Gary Dymski, Jason Ziedenberg, Maura McDermott, Silja Talvi, Adam Shatz, Raj Patel, George Lerner, Karma Waltonen, and the slew of other friends and colleagues with whom I brainstormed over the months, my sincere thanks. You helped keep me on course throughout this journey.

On the editorial front, however, nobody deserves warmer thanks than does my researcher, Caitlin Buckley. Caitlin took to the task of helping me research *Inside Obama's Brain* with relish and great skill. Her daily e-mails, containing phone numbers, book references, summaries of research done, and intimations of research still to come, were continual grist for the mill. And as the manuscript neared completion, her keen editorial eyes proved to be invaluable assets. This volume would have been much the poorer had it not been for Caitlin's presence in the wings.

To all these individuals, as well as to the scores of other

sources and friends not named in these acknowledgments, a hearty "Cheers, mates." Your cooperation and enthusiasm made this book possible.

On a personal level, thanks, again, to my parents, Lenore and Jack, for teaching me the importance of love, curiosity, humility, and laughter; and to my brother, Kolya, and to my sister, Tanya, for being lodestars on the voyage through life. You all have truly made me who I am. To my grandparents, on both sides, "thank you" doesn't even begin to express what I feel for you and for the houses you filled with happiness and love when I was growing up. To my wife, Julie Sze, for tolerating the intrusion of two book projects into our home within a one-year period, I extend my humble thanks. The strains have been huge; my deepest appreciation for making them navigable and, yes, at times even fun. And above all, I owe huge hugs to my five-year-old daughter, Sofia, and to my two-year-old son, Leo. Your ongoing and gleeful chants of "yes we can" throughout the election period and in the months following have truly been joys to the ears.

NOTES

Introduction: Setting the Stage

1. Michael Sokolove, "The Transformation of Levittown," *New York Times*, Nov. 9, 2008.
2. Barack Obama, Grant Park, Chicago, Nov. 4, 2008.
3. Author interview with Jerry Kellman, Jan. 28, 2009.
4. Interview transcript at back of Evan Thomas's book *A Long Time Coming*, PublicAffairs, New York, 2009.
5. The quote is taken from a question-and-answer session, the transcript of which is reprinted at the back of *After Alinsky*, ed. Peg Knoepfle, Sangamon State University, Springfield, Illinois, 1990.
6. Harry Boyte and Sara Evans, *Free Spaces: The Sources of Democratic Change in America*, Harper & Row, New York, 1986, 2.
7. Ibid., 17.
8. Author interview with Marshall Ganz, Feb. 5, 2009.
9. Author interview with Stephen Skowronek, Jan. 16, 2009.
10. Author interview with Douglas Brinkley, Jan. 22, 2009.
11. Butts used this analogy in an interview with *Rolling Stone* reporter Ben

Wallace-Wells, for his article "Destiny's Child," *Rolling Stone* 1020, Feb. 22, 2007.

12. This information was provided the author by an inside source who wished to remain anonymous.

13. Author interview with Charles Halpern, Dec. 28, 2009.

14. Barack Obama, *Dreams from My Father,* Three Rivers Press, New York, 2004, xvi.

15. The event took place on November 23, 2004. It was broadcast on C-SPAN's *Book TV.*

16. Author interview with John Kupper, Jan. 30, 2009.

17. ABC News, Feb. 23, 2009.

Chapter One: Focus

1. Author interview with Loretta Augustine-Herron, Feb. 10, 2009.

2. Author interview with Yvonne Lloyd, Feb. 13, 2009.

3. Author interview with Eric Kusunoki, Jan. 2, 2009.

4. Author interview with Judson Miner, Jan. 24, 2009.

5. Author interview with George Galland, Jan. 27, 2009.

6. Author interview with Elizabeth Hollander, Jan. 22, 2009.

7. Author interview with John Owens, Jan. 15, 2009.

8. Scott Fornek, " 'I've Got a Competitive Nature': Beneath the Rock Star Fame Is a Politician Who Plays Hard to Win, Whether It Be in Scrabble or a Race to Topple an Incumbent," *Chicago Sun-Times,* Oct. 3, 2004. In the article, Maya Soetoro-Ng was quoted as saying "he would crow like a rooster and flap his wings and make slam-dunk motions" when he won at Scrabble.

9. Author interview with Whitman Soule, Feb. 3, 2009.

10. Author interviews with Ruben Wilson, Jan. 18, 2009; and Jahi Hassan, Jan. 18, 2009.

11. Alexander Wolff, "The Audacity of Hoops," Sports Illustrated Online, Jan. 13, 2009.

12. Author interview with Loretta Augustine-Herron, Feb. 10, 2009.

13. This information is from Evan Thomas's book *A Long Time Coming.*

14. Bob Herbert interviewed Obama at the JFK Library and Museum, Boston, Oct. 20, 2006. The event was broadcast by C-SPAN's *Book TV.*

15. Author interview with Toni Preckwinkle, Jan. 26, 2009.

16. Author interview with Jerry Kellman, Jan. 6, 2009.

17. Knoepfle, ed., *After Alinsky,* 36–40.

18. Author interview with Reverend Alvin Love, Feb. 10, 2009.

19. Author interview with Mike Kruglik, Jan. 8, 2009.

20. Author interview with Harry Boyte, Jan. 6, 2009.

21. Author interview with Sanford Newman, Jan. 13, 2009.

22. Gretchen Reynolds, "Vote of Confidence," *Chicago* magazine, Jan. 1993.

23. Author interview with Rachel Klayman, Apr. 10, 2009.

24. Author interview with Alan Dershowitz, Jan. 20, 2009.

25. Author interview with Paul Harstad, Jan. 16, 2009.

26. Author interview with Alan Solomont, Jan. 16, 2009.

27. Author interview with Ken Rolling, Jan. 21, 2009.

28. The source of this information wished to remain anonymous.

Chapter Two: Looking Inward, Reaching Outward

1. Obama, *Dreams from My Father,* xii.

2. Ibid., xi.

3. Maya Soetoro-Ng gave this answer in response to a written question by the author during her appearance at California State University, Sacramento, Mar. 17, 2009.

4. Obama interview with Connie Martinson in August 1995, on *Connie Martinson Talks Books.* Martinson subsequently donated recordings of her interviews to the Claremont University–based Drucker Institute's archives. The archive's Web site is www.druckerinstitute.com/DruckerArchives.aspx.

5. Dan Nakaso, "Obama's Mother's Work Focus of UH Seminar," *Honolulu Advertiser,* Sept. 12, 2008.

6. Janny Scott, "Obama's Mother—an Unconventional Life," *New York Times,* Mar. 14, 2008.

7. Philippe Wamba, *Kinship: A Family's Journey in Africa and America*, Dutton, New York, 1999, 53.

8. Author interview with Douglas Brinkley, Jan. 22, 2009.

9. Wamba, *Kinship*, 76.

10. Author interview with Harry Boyte, Jan. 6, 2009.

11. Barack Obama, "What I Want for You—and Every Child in America," *Parade*, Jan. 14, 2009.

12. Tonya Lewis interview with Michelle Obama, "Your Next First Lady?" *Glamour*, Sept. 3, 2007.

13. Author interview with Senator Kirk Dillard, Jan. 19, 2009.

14. Obama, *Dreams from My Father*, 111.

15. Barack Obama, *The Audacity of Hope*, Vintage, New York, 2008, 64.

16. Ibid., 5.

17. Obama, *Dreams from My Father*, 91.

18. Hannah Pool, "Question Time," *Guardian*, Nov. 16, 2006.

19. Author interview with Jerry Kellman, Jan. 6, 2009.

Chapter Three: Sense of History

1. David Remnick, "The Joshua Generation: Race and the Campaign of Barack Obama," *New Yorker*, Nov. 17, 2008.

2. Frederick Douglass: "What, to the Slave, is the Fourth of July?" A speech given at Corinthian Hall, in Rochester, New York, on July 4, 1852. Quoted in *Great Speeches by African Americans*, ed. James Daley, Dover, Mineola, New York, 2006.

3. Charles Payne, *I've Got the Light of Freedom: The Organizing Tradition and the Mississippi Freedom Struggles*, University of California Press, 1995, 98.

4. Obama, *The Audacity of Hope*, 112.

5. Ibid., 11.

6. Ibid., 68.

7. Obama, "What I Want for You—and Every Child in America."

8. Obama, *Dreams from My Father*, 277.

9. Ted Sorensen, *Counselor: A Life at the Edge of History,* Harper, New York, 2008, 140.

10. Jann Wenner, "A Conversation with Barack Obama," *Rolling Stone* 1056/1057, July 10–24, 2008.

11. Articles in the *New York Times, Los Angeles Times,* and Salon.com have detailed Obama's literary tastes.

12. Author interview with Richard Donohue, Jan. 21, 2009.

13. Author interview with Harry Boyte, Jan. 21, 2009.

14. Harry Boyte and Carmen Sirianni, "Renewing the Democratic Faith: Draft Framework for Civil Engagement Discussion," July 12, 2008.

15. Obama, *Dreams from My Father,* 437.

16. This story was told by radio reporter Amy Goodman during a gathering of journalists in Los Angeles, Apr. 25, 2009.

17. Barack Obama, Knox College Commencement Address, June 4, 2005, quoted in *Great Speeches by African Americans,* ed. James Daley, Dover, Mineola, New York, 2006.

18. Author interview with Reverend Robert Jones, Feb. 12, 2009.

19. Author interview with Ted Sorensen, Feb. 18, 2009.

20. Author interview with Heather Booth, Dec. 31, 2008.

21. This quote was first publicized in 2004, two years after the conversation took place. Ron Suskind, "Without a Doubt," *New York Times,* Oct. 17, 2004.

22. Franklin Delano Roosevelt, State of the Union Address to Congress, Jan. 6, 1941.

23. Ben Wallace-Wells, "Destiny's Child."

24. Obama, *Dreams from My Father,* xi.

25. Obama, *Audacity of Hope,* 330.

Chapter Four: Self-confidence

1. Author interview with Denny Jacobs, Feb. 19, 2009.

2. Tonya Lewis interview with Michelle Obama, "Your Next First Lady?".

3. Author interview with George Galland, Jan. 27, 2009.

4. Author interview with Geoff Stone, Feb. 10, 2009.

5. Author interview with David Wilkins, Mar. 18, 2009.

6. *Washington Post* editorial board meeting, Jan. 15, 2009. A recording of the meeting was posted on the Internet.

7. Boyte and Evans, *Free Spaces*, 6–7.

8. David Mendell, *Obama: From Promise to Power*, Amistad paperback edition, New York, October 2008, 7.

9. Ibid.

10. Author interview with John Cameron, Jan. 29, 2009.

11. Author interview with Jacky Grimshaw, Feb. 14, 2009.

12. Ted Kleine, "Bobby Rush's Enemies Smell Blood," *Chicago Reader*, Mar. 17, 2000.

13. Author interview with John Kupper, Jan. 28, 2009.

14. Author interview with Mike Kruglik, Jan. 8, 2009.

15. Obama, *Audacity of Hope*, 126, 130.

16. Author interview with Jacky Grimshaw, Feb. 14, 2009.

17. Author interview with Reverend Alvin Love, Feb. 10, 2009.

18. The source of this information wished to remain anonymous.

19. Author interview with Leon Despres, Feb. 12, 2009.

Chapter Five: Poise

1. Author interview with Jackie Kendall, Jan. 16, 2009.

2. Author interview with John Milner, Jan. 14, 2009.

3. Author interview with Mary Gonzalez, Jan. 27, 2009.

4. Author interviews with Stephen Heintz, Jan. 12, 2009; and with Charles Halpern, Dec. 28, 2009.

5. Author interview with David Wilkins, Mar. 18, 2009.

6. Author interview with Linda Randle, Feb. 4, 2009.

7. The sources for the information in this paragraph wished to remain anonymous.

8. Author interview with David Friedman, Jan. 13, 2009.

9. Mariana Cook, "A Couple in Chicago," *New Yorker*, Jan. 19, 2009. Based on an interview Cook conducted with the Obamas on May 26, 1996.

10. Information provided author during interview with Hill Harper, one of the participants in the basketball game, Jan. 22, 2009.

Case Study: Tackling Race Head-on

1. "The Future of Urban Centers: What Are the Policy Options?" an American Enterprise Institute–sponsored roundtable, moderated by John Charles Daly, Jan. 27, 1978.

2. Quoted in the question-and-answer session transcripts in *After Alinsky*.

3. Author interview with Judson Miner, Jan. 24, 2009.

4. Author interview with David Wilkins, Mar. 18, 2009.

5. Author interview with Julianne Malveaux, Feb. 2, 2009.

6. Obama interview with Connie Martinson, on *Connie Martinson Talks Books*, August 1995.

7. Janny Scot, "Obama Chose Reconciliation Over Rancor," *New York Times*, Mar. 18, 2008.

8. Author interview with Charles Halpern, Dec. 28, 2008.

9. Obama, *Dreams from My Father*, 82.

Chapter Six: Curiosity

1. Author interview with George Galland, Jan. 27, 2009.

2. Jann Wenner, "A Conversation with Barack Obama."

3. Barack Obama, *Dreams from My Father*, xii.

4. Maya Soetoro-Ng, speech at California State University, Sacramento, Mar. 17, 2009.

5. The source for this information is an author interview with Obama's high school friend Mitch Kam, Jan. 13, 2009.

6. Obama, *Dreams from My Father*, 100.

7. Author interview with Roger Boesche, Feb. 18, 2009.

8. Author interview with Elizabeth Hollander, Jan. 22, 2009.

9. Amanda Griscom Little, "The Freshman," *Rolling Stone* 964/965, Dec. 30, 2004.

10. Author interview with Robin Kelley, Jan. 24, 2009.

11. Author interview with Richard Donohue, Jan. 21, 2009.

12. Author interview with Douglas Brinkley, Jan. 22, 2009.

13. Walt Whitman, *Complete Prose Works*, D. McKay, Philadelphia, 1891. The quote is from page 502, in a chapter titled "Good-bye My Fancy," the second annex to *Leaves of Grass*.

14. Obama, *Dreams from My Father*, 122.

15. Author interview with Reverend Alvin Love, Feb. 10, 2009.

16. Author interview with Senator Bill Haine, Feb. 19, 2009.

17. Jeff Johnson, "What's In It for Us? Barack Obama and the Black Vote," Black Entertainment Television, www.bet.com/ONTV/ontv_betnewsspecial_barackobama.html.

18. Author interview with Abner Mikva, Feb. 12, 2009.

19. Obama was speaking on his book, *Dreams from My Father*, at a New York City Barnes & Noble, Nov. 23, 2004. The event was broadcast on C-SPAN's *Book TV*.

20. James Cone, *Black Theology and Black Power*, Seabury Press, New York, 1969, 111. According to Jody Kretzmann, Cone was one of the authors the young community organizer Obama read.

21. Obama, *The Audacity of Hope*, 328.

22. Author interview with Reverend Robert Jones, Feb. 12, 2009.

23. Obama, *Dreams from My Father*, 261.

24. Ibid., 294.

25. Ali is quoted by Davis Miller, *The Tao of Muhammad Ali*, Three Rivers Press, New York, 1999, 253.

26. This information was reported by J. Patrick Coolican in "Obama Goes Gloves Off, Head-On," *Las Vegas Sun*, Jan. 14, 2008.

27. This information is contained in Evan Thomas's book *A Long Time Coming*.

28. Obama, *Dreams from My Father,* 427.

29. Author interview with Marshall Ganz, Feb. 5, 2009.

Chapter Seven: Thinking Outside the Box

1. Maya Soetoro-Ng speech at California State University, Sacramento, Mar. 17, 2009.

2. Michiko Kakutani, "Obama's Foursquare Politics, with a Dab of Dijon," *New York Times,* Oct. 17, 2006.

3. Zadie Smith, "Speaking in Tongues." The lecture was reprinted in the *New York Review of Books,* Feb. 26, 2009.

4. Author interview with Rachel Klayman, Apr. 10, 2009.

5. Author interview with Douglas Brinkley, Jan. 22, 2009.

6. Author interview with Mary Gonzalez, Jan. 27, 2009.

7. Author interview with Jim Capraro, Jan. 13, 2009.

8. Author interview with Marshall Ganz, Feb. 5, 2009.

9. Author interview with Galuzzo's wife Mary Gonzalez, who was also present at the interaction, Jan. 27, 2009.

10. Author interview with William McNary, Jan. 15, 2009.

11. Author interview with Jody Kretzmann, Jan. 8, 2009.

12. Barack Obama, "Why Organize?" in *After Alinsky.*

13. Author interview with Hill Harper, Jan. 22, 2009.

14. The Obama-McCain discussion at Saddleback church was broadcast on CNN, http://www.cnn.com/2008/POLITICS/08/16/warren.forum/#cnnSTCVideo.

15. Obama, *Dreams from My Father,* 11–12.

16. Ibid., 12.

17. Obama posited this explanation for why he went into community organizing during his interview with Connie Martinson, on *Connie Martinson Talks Books,* August 1995.

18. Author interviews with Al Kindle, Jan. 27 and 30, 2009.

19. Author interview with Linda Randle, Feb. 4, 2009.

20. Author interview with Abner Mikva, Feb. 12, 2009.

21. Author's e-mail correspondence with Laurence Tribe, Feb. 24, 2009.

22. Irving Howe, *World of Our Fathers: The Journey of the East European Jews to America and the Life They Found and Made,* Touchstone, New York, 1976, 27. The immigrant being quoted was named Mary Antin.

23. Barack Obama, Knox College Commencement Address.

24. Barack Obama, *Change We Can Believe In: Barack Obama's Plan to Renew America's Promise,* Three Rivers Press, New York, 2008, 14.

25. Author interview with Harry Boyte, Jan. 6, 2009.

26. Hank de Zutter, "What Makes Obama Run?" *Chicago Reader,* Dec. 8, 1995.

Chapter Eight: The Smooth Politician

1. Author interview with David Wilkins, Mar. 18, 2009.

2. Author interview with Douglas Baird, Feb. 5, 2009.

3. Harry Boyte and Steven Hahn, "Obama Picks Up the Message That RFK Popularized," *Star Tribune,* June 4, 2008.

4. De Zutter, "What Makes Obama Run?"

5. Author interview with Stephen Heintz, Jan. 12, 2009.

6. Obama, *The Audacity of Hope,* 250.

7. Author interview with Chris Edley, Feb. 9, 2009.

8. Tammerlin Drummond, "Barack Obama's Law Personality," *Los Angeles Times,* Mar. 19, 1990.

9. Author interview with John Milner, Jan. 14, 2009.

10. http://firstread.msnbc.msn.com/archive/2008/05/29/1076277.aspx.

11. Eric Bates, "Obama's Moment," *Rolling Stone* 1064, Oct. 30, 2008.

12. Author interview with Stephen Heintz, Jan. 12, 2009.

13. Author interview with Ken Rolling, Jan. 21, 2009.

14. Author interview with Reverend Alvin Love, Feb. 10, 2009.

15. Author interview with John Kupper, Jan. 28, 2009.

16. Adler is quoted in David Krasner's *Method Acting Reconsidered: Theory, Practice, Future.* Revised edition, MacMillan, New York, 2000, 4.

17. The 2008 promotional brochure for Mayor Daley quotes Obama as making this statement on Jan. 22, 2007.

18. Author interview with Ken Rolling, Jan. 21, 2009.

19. Author interview with Toni Preckwinkle, Jan. 26, 2009.

20. Author interview with Senator Rickey Hendon, Feb. 3, 2009.

21. "*National Journal*'s 2007 Vote Ratings," *National Journal,* Jan. 31, 2008.

22. David Leonhardt, "After the Great Recession," *New York Times Magazine,* May 3, 2009.

23. Author interview with Reverend Alvin Love, Feb. 10, 2009.

Case Study: The Iowa Caucus

1. Author interview with David Yepsen, Jan. 14, 2009.

2. Author interview with Jason Clayworth, Feb. 24, 2009.

3. Author interview with John Kupper, Jan. 28, 2009.

4. Author interview with John Kupper, Mar. 3, 2009.

5. Author interview with Marshall Ganz, Feb. 5, 2009.

6. Data can be found in *How Barack Obama Won: A State-by-State Guide to the Historic 2008 Presidential Election,* Chuck Todd and Sheldon Gawiser, Vintage, New York, 2009, 70. Edwards received 29.7 percent and Clinton 29.5 percent.

Chapter Nine: The Inspirer

1. Barack Obama, "Why Organize?" in *After Alinsky,* ed. Peg Knoepfle, Sangamon State University, Springfield, Illinois, 1990.

2. Author interview with Bettylu Saltzman, Feb. 5, 2009.

3. Author interview with Whitman Soule, Feb. 3, 2009.

4. Harry Boyte, "Civil Agency and the Politics of Knowledge," Kettering Foundation, Dayton, Ohio, forthcoming.

5. 2006 Book Expo America, June 23, 2006. The panel was moderated by author Marie Arana. The speakers were Barack Obama, John Updike,

and Amy Sedaris. The event was podcast at: http://bookexpocast .com/2006/06/23/bea-12-saturday-book-author-breakfast/.

6. Hill Harper, *Letters to a Young Brother,* Gotham Books, New York, 2006, 157.

7. Obama used this phrase in a conversation with *New York Times* columnist Bob Herbert, at the John F. Kennedy Library and Museum in Boston, Oct. 20, 2006. Broadcast on C-SPAN's *Book TV.*

8. Miller, *The Tao of Muhammad Ali,* 80.

9. Author interview with Loretta Augustine-Herron, Feb. 10, 2009.

10. Author interview with Yvonne Lloyd, Feb. 13, 2009.

11. Saul Alinsky, *Reveille for Radicals,* University of Chicago Press, Chicago, 1946, 80.

12. Adam Nagourney and Marjorie Connelly, "Poll Finds Faith in Obama, Mixed with Patience," *New York Times,* Jan. 18, 2009.

13. Author interview with Troy Duster, Jan. 25, 2009.

Case Study: Team of Rivals Redux

1. Doris Kearns Goodwin, *Team of Rivals: The Political Genius of Abraham Lincoln,* Simon & Schuster, 2006, xvii.

2. Ibid., 318.

3. http://www.publicbroadcasting.net/netradio/arts.artsmain?action =viewArticle&sid=17&pid=283&id=1471706.

4. Author interview with Sanford Newman, Jan. 13, 2009.

5. Author interview with John Kupper, Mar. 3, 2009.

6. Author interview with Richard Donohue, Jan. 21, 2009.

7. Author interview with Geoff Stone, Feb. 10, 2009.

8. Author interview with Chris Edley, Feb. 9, 2009.

Chapter Ten: The Leader

1. Author interview with Bill Haine, Feb. 19, 2009.

2. Author interview with Eric Garcetti, Feb. 24, 2009.

3. Author interview with Bill Haine, Feb. 19, 2009.

4. Author interview with John Owens, Jan. 15, 2009.

5. Saul Alinsky, *Rules for Radicals: A Practical Primer for Realistic Radicals,* Random House, New York, 1971, xxiii.

6. Author interview with Patricia Graham, Feb. 3, 2009.

7. Author interview with John Trasviña, Feb. 18, 2009.

8. Author interview with Denny Jacobs, Feb. 19, 2009.

9. New York, Barnes & Noble, Nov. 23, 2004. The event was broadcast on C-SPAN's *Book TV.*

10. Conversation with *New York Times* columnist Bob Herbert, at Boston's JFK Library and Museum, Oct. 20, 2006. Broadcast on C-SPAN's *Book TV.*

11. Author interview with Ted Sorensen, Feb. 18, 2009.

Conclusion: A New Morning

1. Rep. Lynn Westmoreland, of Georgia, made the comment in Washington, D.C., in early September 2008.

2. MSNBC interview with Tom Brokaw and General Colin Powell, Oct. 19, 2008.

3. Langston Hughes, "Let America Be America Again," 1938.

4. Author interview with Governor Cuomo, Jan. 12, 2009.

INDEX